KIDS AROUND THE COUNTRY
WRITE THEIR OWN
WACKY HUMOR

A seven-year-old in Los Angeles defined the Depression as "a long time ago when instead of people becoming millionaires, millionaires became people."

A girl whose imagination was stronger than her desire to study wrote "The pistol of a flower is its only protection against insects."

A boy wrote "If conditions are not favorable, bacteria go into a period of adolescence."

from "Those Funny Kids"
by Dick Van Dyke

MORE TALES OUT OF SCHOOL

D0874891

to Mark,
a friend &
colleague,

MORE TALES
OUT OF SCHOOL

Edited by
Helen S. Weiss
and
M. Jerry Weiss

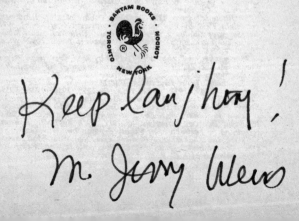

Keep laughing!
M. Jerry Weiss

RL 7, IL 7+

MORE TALES OUT OF SCHOOL
A Bantam Book / May 1980

ISBN 0–553–13546–5

COPYRIGHT NOTICES AND ACKNOWLEDGMENTS

To students and teachers who continue
to demonstrate the joys of laughter

The decent docent doesn't doze:
He teaches standing on his toes.
His student dassn't doze—and does,
And that's what teaching is and was.

David McCord

Contents

Introduction

Once upon a time, a teacher asked a student to explain "These are the times that try men's souls." The student replied instantly, "They are the seconds, the minutes, the hours, the days, the weeks, the months, the terms, the years of schooling, sometimes referred to as academic calendars."

Once upon a time, a student in a Pennsylvania high school challenged his math teacher by asking, "Why must we take plane geometry?" The teacher very seriously replied, "If the Nile River ever overflows, you'll be able to find your boundary."

Once upon a time, a school board decided to ask students who had graduated from a particular high school in that school district to evaluate the effectiveness of the school curriculum on their lives. One alumna replied, "My biology course, with the detailed laboratory workbook, and the teacher, who required the students to memorize all the parts of the body and the various systems that operate within the human being, prepared me, at best, to understand television programs such as *The Doctors* and *Marcus Welby* and to perform self-surgery."

Exam question: "Explain Missouri Compromise."

Student reply: "I didn't know she did."

Once upon a time, a psychology professor would ask, "Will all of the students who are absent today please stop by my desk on your way out?" The same scholarly person would often emphasize certain points by rapping several times on the desk, and upon hearing the knocking, would turn to the door and call out, "Come on in."

At one major university, a professor, teaching a June inter-session course, was involved in his lecture when the class softly giggled and chuckled. Completely baffled, the professor subtly checked to see if his shoes matched, if his socks matched, if his zipper was zipped. Finding nothing wrong, he continued the lecture, but from time to time, the subdued outbreaks occurred. Finally, he realized the cause. Instead of referring to "this inter-session course," he had been saying "this intercourse session." What a difference word sequence can make!

Each of the above stories is true. Parents, teachers, and students often can recall those very special moments in school when the unexpected happens. How precious are those moments when classrooms are filled with laughter, whether it is planned or accidental.

More Tales Out of School is a collection of such moments, funny stories, poems, cartoons, essays, and anecdotes about school situations and parent-child-teacher relationships that point out that silence is not necessarily synonymous with learning. Much learning does take place amid the sounds of laughter. What's wrong with encouraging children to laugh? The sacred halls of academia, often viewed in so solemn and somber a manner, should ring with laughter from time to time. Neither teachers nor students can afford to overlook the wits who have a way of putting people, places, and events in a rather special perspective.

Humor not only entertains, but it also provokes and/or evokes critical thinking. All humans have emotions to give them pleasure and to allow them to express themselves. The humorists are "the punchers" and "the punched." They portray themselves as winners and as losers. Some create hilarious, sometimes painful, sometimes compassionate, situations in which others are victimized; some make themselves the victims of circumstances that defy the most logical explanations and the best laid plans. In reacting to humor, don't try to explain or justify your feelings. The talented humorist who reaches you, the reader, has magical powers and a very special way with language and/or pictures.

Each section of this book is self-explanatory. Every stage of schooling is included in the anthology. A variety of humorous forms has been selected to show the gamut of education, from preschool through basic adult education. The writers represent the most successful contemporary humorists.

H. Allen Smith, Dick Van Dyke, and Andrew Summers share the humor of real children in many classrooms.

The school memories of Will Rogers, Sam Levenson, and Peter Ustinov are expressed in their autobiographical recollections. It could be interesting to compare the views today's students have about school with the hindsight views of these authors.

Humor abounds in poetry. Each poet, with a unique style, uses the pen to provide a variety of attitudes and experiences about schools and learning.

Every aspect of academia is fair target for the satirists. Richard Armour and George Boas zero in on academic types with hilarious precision. Woody Allen sees school schedules from his own delightfully peculiar perspective.

Erma Bombeck, Jean Kerr, and Art Buchwald emphasize the families' points of view.

Fran Leibowitz reveals a glimpse of doctrine she acquired in school along with a talent for chart listing.

And school will never be the same when students follow the advice offered by Delia Ephron, *The National Lampoon,* and *Mad* magazine.

This thematic presentation of schools should tempt many to put their schooling in a proper perspective. Parents, students, teachers, and administrators are all part of a unique establishment that prepares people to find out what they know or don't know; what they want or don't want; what they need or don't need; what they have or don't have; or, better yet, how to get what they don't have. Some selections will appear absolutely absurd, yet plausible; others may cause one to sit back and to shriek, "Someone wrote this about me!"

It's important to realize that practically everybody who reads from this book has had some schooling. Remember also that even humorists have been students. They are a courageous lot to take on learning, learners, and the learned to show how so many have become so concerned with triumphing over trivia.

So just when you feel the world is caving in because the homework's not done, the book's not read, the report's not written, the notes have not been committed to immortal or immoral memory, why not laugh?

KIDS THEMSELVES

Those Funny Kids
Dick Van Dyke

A Brooklyn teacher was asked by a Chinese boy, "Are you Italian?" "Yes," she said. The boy turned to a Black classmate and said, "I told you—all Italians look alike."

No one gets stared at more than a teacher who fills in for a day or two. While substituting for a red-haired music teacher, a young woman in West Dundee, Illinois, realized that a first-grade girl had been watching her every move all week. Finally the little girl couldn't stand the suspense any longer and asked, "What did you do with Mrs. Paul's red hair?"

A French teacher in New York was subbing one day in a high school class when a student walked in and asked, "Are you the refill?"

A boy in East Rockaway, New York, was sure he knew the name of the President who led us out of the Depression: "Franklin D. Roosevelt Drive." (His teacher was tempted to ask him if the father of our country was the George Washington Bridge.)

After telling her kindergarteners about the first Thanksgiving, a teacher in Queens, New York, asked, "Who remembers the name of the boat that brought the Pilgrims to America?" A boy answered, "The *Cauliflower*."

During an eighth-grade history class in Visalia, California, a student was asked to write a character sketch of Miles Standish. He gave this response: "When it came to war, Miles was a brave and honest man. But when it came to love, he was like a second grader doing eighth-grade work."

Another favorite children's character in history is the man who discovered America, known to at least one youngster as "Misterpher Columbus." Another boy in La Porte, Indiana, who is obviously a TV fan, thought the man was "Columbo."

A seven-year-old in Okemos, Michigan, balked at the notion that Columbus had shown our planet is round. "I don't believe the earth is round," he said, "because everybody always talks about going to the four corners of it."

The day after hearing about Columbus, a first grader in Garland, Texas, ran up to his teacher and said, "I remember the names of his ships . . . the Nina, the Pinta, and the Toyota."

On the birthday of a famous composer, the Holy Cross School in Omaha had the custom of piping his music throughout the school at lunchtime. After the children heard the "Hallelujah Chorus" from Handel's *Messiah,* a Sister asked her class to tell whose birthday they were celebrating. A boy yelled, "George Frederic Doorknob!"

Here are a few more slightly off-key observations from music historians of uncertain note:

"My favorite composer is Opus."

"Gregory (of the famous chant) lived from 540 to 604, but I forget whether it was AC or DC."

"My best-loved piece is the Bronze Lullaby."

"Henry Purcell is a well-known composer few people have ever heard of."

Seeking that famous quote about having but one life to give for his country, a history teacher in East Rockaway, New York, asked the class:

"What was the last thing Nathan Hale said before being hung as an American spy?"

The answer: "Help!"

During a lesson on William Tell, a teacher in Winston-Salem asked, "What is the difference between being born of gentle birth, and born of peasant birth?"

A girl from a large family volunteered, "One is when you have the doctor, and the other is when you don't."

A seven-year-old in Los Angeles defined the Depression as "a long time ago when instead of people becoming millionaires, millionaires became people."

Nothing lightens a teacher's task at paper-grading time more than an occasional blooper, like these from examinations:

What was the Industrial Revolution?
"It was the change from Reproduction in the home to Reproduction in the factory."

Name two hardships endured by the South during the Civil War.
"The *Monitor* and the *Merrimac*."

Define the term "to bear arms."
"You may wear sleeveless dresses."

What is Democracy?
"Democracy is that system of government where

one man is as good as the next, and sometimes a lot better."

What was the first permanent settlement made by the Europeans in Florida?
"Miami Beach."

The Incans used what animals for wool?
"Woolves."

Essay writers produced off-center answers like these:

"The blocks of stone used to build the pyramids in ancient Egypt were dragged up the ramp by sheer union labor."

"Greek fighters would wrestle until one conceived."

"During the French Revolution, excessive murders were committed on each person."

"The Russian peasants lived in mud huts with lots of rough mating on the floor."

"The workers all worked very hard, but all the money they made went to fill the coiffures of the wealthy."

"Cyrus McCormick invented the raper and put thousands of men out of work."

"I like Thomas à Becket best because he loved his people. He was a brilliant and wonderful man. His own dear friends killed him."

A teacher of fourth graders in La Feria, Texas, told the class about an eclipse of the moon that night at ten, suggesting that perhaps their parents would let them stay up late and watch. A boy immediately asked, "Which channel?"

A teacher in Salt Lake City asked her class, "How can astronomers tell the difference between a star and a planet?" A boy replied, "A star has five points."

In closing this potpourri of science, here are some examination bloopers which show young minds working away, *almost* coming up with the right answers. . . .

A boy wrote, "If conditions are not favorable, bacteria go into a period of adolescence."

A girl whose imagination was stronger than her desire to study wrote, "The pistol of a flower is its only protection against insects."

And here are some question and answer exchanges:

Name a prehistoric mammal which was characterized by long upper canine teeth.
"The save a tooth tiger."

Give an example of a disease caused by yeasts.
"Alcoholism."

Describe the food chain.
"A bunch of grocery stores."

What animal has the highest level of intelligence?
"A giraffe."

Name four synthetic fibers.
"Acetate, nylon, rayon, and crayon."

And lastly, here are a few other scientific observations you may not have heard until now. . . .

"Glass will change shape while in heat."

"Without the law of gravity, people would be afraid to move about for fear they would just fly away."

"One of the most controversial drugs is pot, or, as it is medically known, grass."

How do birds help the farmers?
"They help the farmer to eat the insects."

Describe a Thesaurus.

"I never seen one, but I know they all died a long time ago."

Who founded New York City?
"Christopher Columbus. He was looking for India when he founded us instead."

The Downfall of Rome
H. Allen Smith

Great stacks of books have been written by people in an effort to explain why Rome fell. Scholarly historians have devoted their whole lives to the question, yet none of them ever really arrived at a more sensible answer than that contained in a penciled manuscript unearthed in Greenwich, Connecticut, one day in 1948. It was the work of a nine-year-old boy and follows:

THE DOWNFALL OF ROME
The Downfall of Rome was caused by carelessness.

That sapient bit of historical analysis found its way eventually into the pages of the *New Yorker*, a sort of clearing house for the finest writing produced by American children. Parents and teachers all over the land, whenever they come upon a bit of juvenilia which they consider pretty close to immortal, think immediately of the *New Yorker*. A parent in Indianapolis, for example, sent in an essay written on assignment by a seventh-grader, as follows:

WHY I WANT TO BE IN THE EIGHTH GRADE

There are not many reason why I want to be in the Eighth Grade.

And a nine-year-old boy won his first literary prize for the following composition:

MANNERS

I have good manners. I say good night and good morning and hello and goodbye, and when I see dead things lying around the house I bury them.

Verbs
Edited by Andrew Summers

What I wont most is strong verbs. Teachers all say I got weak verbs. I got no strong verbs. I always have a tuff time in school cause of that. I been p ushed aroun and hounded to much aboit them verbs. Always then verbs! If I git strong verbs may-bee teachers will leaf me alone. Other that that I wood like probly a hamboger and da malt. Porter sez he eat at 1215. Do I eat at 1215 are 1230? I steal dont now when I eat?

~~~~~~

I have Always Wanted to be a Philosifer for exra credit

Edited by Andrew Summers

~~~~~~

I have always wanted to be kinda of a philosifer. I would just sit around saying wise and pithy things. My dad likes to say wise and pithy things. He is kinda of a philosifer. He doesn't like to work and would rather sit and drink a lot and read and make lots of comments on things in general. He is a great man and known the answer to a lot of questions and problems. No one ever listens to him though. He has traveled a whole lot. Every now and then he leaves home for several months on a trip. His friends are what some people call Bums. But Bums are usully really philosifers. Dad has a friend who graduated from Yale. Hes the one who taught me the value of wise and pithy sayings and of books. Dad thinks more of nowledge than of work. He also likes poetry.

SCHOOL DAYS

Sick
Shel Silverstein

"I cannot go to school today,"
Said little Peggy Ann McKay.
"I have the measles and the mumps,
A gash, a rash and purple bumps.
My mouth is wet, my throat is dry,
I'm going blind in my right eye.
My tonsils are as big as rocks,
I've counted sixteen chicken pox
And there's one more—that's seventeen,
And don't you think my face looks green?
My leg is cut, my eyes are blue—
It might be instamatic flu.
I cough and sneeze and gasp and choke,
I'm sure that my left leg is broke—
My hip hurts when I move my chin,

My belly button's caving in,
My back is wrenched, my ankle's sprained,
My 'pendix pains each time it rains.
My nose is cold, my toes are numb,
I have a sliver in my thumb.
My neck is stiff, my spine is weak,
I hardly whisper when I speak.
My tongue is filling up my mouth,
I think my hair is falling out.
My elbow's bent, my spine ain't straight,
My temperature is one-o-eight,
My brain is shrunk, I cannot hear,
There is a hole inside my ear.
I have a hangnail, and my heart is—what?
What's that? What's that you say?
You say today is . . . Saturday?
G'bye, I'm going out to play!"

Chester
Shel Silverstein

Chester come to school and said,
"Durn, I growed another head."
Teacher said, "It's time you knowed
The word is 'grew' instead of 'growed.' "

Illegal Possession of Junk Food
Erma Bombeck

A grade school principal in the East became so upset about the lack of nutrition in the lunches the children were eating that he declared an edict banning junk food from the cafeteria.

I have a feeling the kids jammed the edict between two potato chips and two squares of Hershey chocolate and had it for lunch.

There is certainly no quarrel with the theory. Children should eat nutritionally balanced meals. But children do not take to ultimatums. I would have tried the old Accentuate-the-negative-reverse-the-positive-and-make-the-kid-think-your-idea-is-his-and-he's-driving-you-crazy approach.

Instead of an edict, the bulletin would have read something like this:

Memo to: School Children
Re: Nutritional Lunches

1. Carrots are illegal on school premises. Children bringing them from home will need a note from a parent giving permission to have them, or they will be confiscated by the office and held until dismissal time.

2. Locker inspection for thermoses containing hot vegetable soup or other nutritious dishes will be held periodically without warning. At that time, students are instructed to go to their lockers and stand at attention. DO NOT UNLOCK YOUR LOCKER UNTIL A TEACHER INSTRUCTS YOU TO DO SO. Thermoses will be destroyed by the custodian.

3. Because of student demand, we are selling fresh fruit by the door in the cafeteria. This is on a trial basis. If we find this is all students are having for lunch it will be discontinued. Remember, the fruit contains sugar and Billy Tooth is watching you. To avoid congestion at fruit counter, please have correct change.

4. Teachers have reported to the office that raisin boxes and milk cartons have been found on the school grounds. We know there are students who have been sneaking nutritious foods on the premises and for this reason students have been posted and are instructed to "take names."

5. Your principal will be patrolling the lunchroom where he wants to see potato chips, candy bars, tortilla chips, soft drinks, and ice cream. Remember, junk foods build soft bones, soft teeth, and make you sleep a lot.

Trust me, it will work.

~~~~~~

The Autobiography of Will Rogers
Donald Day

~~~~~~

My father was pretty well fixed, and I being the only male son he tried terribly hard to make something out of me. He sent me to about every school in that part of the country. In some of them I would last for three or four months. I got just as far as the fourth reader when the teachers wouldn't seem to be running the school right, and rather than have the school stop I would generally leave.

Then I would start in at another school, tell them I had just finished the third reader and was ready for the fourth. Well, I knew all this fourth grade by heart, so the teacher would remark:

"I never see you studying, yet you seem to know your lessons." I had that education thing figured down to a fine point. Three years in McGuffey's Fourth Reader, and I knew more about it than McGuffey did.

But I don't want any enterprising youth to get the idea that I had the right dope on it. I have regretted all my life that I did not at least take a chance on the fifth grade. It would certainly come in handy right now, and I never go through a day that I am not sorry for the idea I had of how to go to school and not learn anything.

I was just a thinking what I would have to do if I was to start out to help out my old schools. "Drumgoul" was a little one-room log cabin four miles east of Chelsea, Indian Territory (where I am right now writing). It was all Indian kids went there and I being part Cherokee had enough white in me to make my honesty questionable.

There must have been about thirty of us in that room that had rode horseback and walked miles to get there, and by the way it was a Co Ed Institution. About half of em was Coo-Coo Eds. We graduated when we could print our full names and enumerate to the teacher, or Principle or Faculty (well, whenever we could name to her), the nationality of the last Democratic President.

But as I say the school went out of business. We wasent able to get games which was profitable. It seems that other school grabbed off all the other good dates, and got the breaks in the newspapers. We couldent seem to ever be accused of professionalism. I could see the finish even as far back as when I was there along in 1887.

Why I can remember when the Coach couldent get enough out of us 15 Boys out to make a team. We got to running Horse Races instead. I had a little chestnut mare that was beating everything that any of them could ride to school and I was losing interest in what we was really there for. I was kinder forgetting that we was there to put the old school on a Paying basis by seeing how many times we could get through that Goal with that old pigskin.

I got to thinking well Horseracing is the big game, thats where the money is, thats what the crowds pay to see. But as years went along it showed that I was a Lad of mighty poor foresight. Little did I dream that it was football that was to be the real McCoy. Course we had no way of hardly telling it then, for we was paid practically nothing at all. In fact we had what I would call a Real Simon Pure Amateur Team. Course we got our side line (Schooling) free. The Cherokee Nation (we then had our own Government and the name Oklahoma was as foreign to us as a Tooth Paste), well, the Cherokee Nation paid the Teacher.

But anyhow there was a mighty few of us that was there under any kind of a guarantee. Course I will admit one of the Alumni got me to go there. He had spent three weeks there and couldent get along with the Teacher and he wanted to do what he could for the old School so he procured me. I looked like a promising End. I could run pretty fast. In fact my nickname was and is to this day among some of the old-timers "Rabbit." I could never figure out if that referred to my speed or my heart.

Mind you, you wouldent believe it, but we dident even have a Stadium. Think of that in this day and time! Thousands and Thousands of acres surrounded us with not a thing on it but Cows and not a concrete seat for a spectator to sit on. Well you see as I look back on it now, a school like that dident have any license to exist. It had to perish. It just staid with books such as Rays Arithemetic and McGuffey 1st, 2nd, and 2 pupils in the 3rd Readers. We had a Geography around there but we just used it for the pictures of the cattle grazing in the Argentine and the wolves attacking the sleighs in Russia.

Well, you see they just couldent see what was the future in Colleges. They just wore out the old books instead of wearing out some footballs. We had Indian Boys that could knock a Squirrel out of a Tree with a rock. But do you think the Regents knew enough to get a Pop Warner and teach em how to hide a Ball under their Jerseys? No. They just had the old-fashioned idea that the place must be made self-sustaining by learning alone, and you see where their ignorance got them. Now the weeds is higher there than the School house was and thats what is happening in a few places in this country. We got those same "Drumgoul" ideas. Course not many but a few. They wont switch and get to the new ideas that its open field running that gets your old College somewhere and not a pack of spectacled Orators or a mess of Civil Engineers. Its better to turn out one good Coach than Ten College Presidents. His name will be in the papers every day and it will always be referred to where he come from. But with the College Presidents, why as far as publicity is concerned they just as well might have matriculated in Hong Kong. So dont let your school be another Drumgoul.

Mrs. Gorf
Louis Sachar

~~~~~~

Mrs. Gorf had a long tongue and pointed ears. She was the meanest teacher in Wayside School. She taught the class on the thirtieth story.

"If you children are bad," she warned, "or if you answer a problem wrong, I'll wiggle my ears, stick out my tongue, and turn you into apples!" Mrs. Gorf didn't like children, but she loved apples.

Joe couldn't add. He couldn't even count. But he knew that if he answered a problem wrong, he would be turned into an apple. So he copied from John. He didn't like to cheat, but Mrs. Gorf had never taught him how to add.

One day Mrs. Gorf caught Joe copying John's paper. She wiggled her ears—first her right one, then her left—stuck out her tongue, and turned Joe into an apple. Then she turned John into an apple for letting Joe cheat.

"Hey, that isn't fair," said Todd. "John was only trying to help a friend."

Mrs. Gorf wiggled her ears—first her right one, then her left—stuck out her tongue, and turned Todd into an apple. "Does anybody else have an opinion?" she asked.

Nobody said a word.

Mrs. Gorf laughed and placed the three apples on her desk.

Stephen started to cry. He couldn't help it. He was scared.

"I do not allow crying in the classroom," said Mrs. Gorf. She wiggled her ears—first her right one, then her left—stuck out her tongue, and turned Stephen into an apple.

For the rest of the day, the children were absolutely quiet. And when they went home, they were too scared even to talk to their parents.

But Joe, John, Todd, and Stephen couldn't go home. Mrs. Gorf just left them on her desk. They were able to talk to each other, but they didn't have much to say.

Their parents were very worried. They didn't know where their children were. Nobody seemed to know.

The next day Kathy was late for school. As soon as she walked in, Mrs. Gorf turned her into an apple.

Paul sneezed during class. He was turned into an apple.

Nancy said, "God bless you!" when Paul sneezed. Mrs. Gorf wiggled her ears—first her right one, then her left—stuck out her tongue, and turned Nancy into an apple.

Terrence fell out of his chair. He was turned into an apple.

Maurecia tried to run away. She was halfway to the door as Mrs. Gorf's right ear began to wiggle. When she reached the door, Mrs. Gorf's left ear wiggled. Maurecia opened the door and had one foot outside when Mrs. Gorf stuck out her tongue. Maurecia became an apple.

Mrs. Gorf picked up the apple from the floor and put it on her desk with the others. Then a funny thing happened. Mrs. Gorf turned around and fell over a piece of chalk.

The three Erics laughed. They were turned into apples.

Mrs. Gorf had a dozen apples on her desk: Joe, John, Todd, Stephen, Kathy, Paul, Nancy, Terrence, Maurecia, and the three Erics—Eric Fry, Eric Bacon, and Eric Ovens.

Louis, the yard teacher, walked into the classroom. He had missed the children at recess. He had heard that Mrs. Gorf was a mean teacher. So he came up to investigate. He saw the twelve apples on Mrs. Gorf's desk. "I must be wrong," he thought. "She must be a good teacher if so many children bring her apples." He walked back down to the playground.

The next day a dozen more children were turned into apples. Louise, the yard teacher, came back into the room. He saw twenty-four apples on Mrs. Gorf's desk. There were only three children left in the class. "She must be the best teacher in the world," he thought.

By the end of the week all of the children were apples. Mrs. Gorf was very happy. "Now I can go home," she said. "I don't have to teach any more. I won't have to walk up thirty flights of stairs ever again."

"You're not going anywhere," shouted Todd. He jumped off the desk and bopped Mrs. Gorf on the nose. The rest of the apples followed. Mrs. Gorf fell on the floor. The apples jumped all over her.

"Stop," she shouted, "or I'll turn you into applesauce!"

But the apples didn't stop, and Mrs. Gorf could do nothing about it.

"Turn us back into children," Todd demanded.

Mrs. Gorf had no choice. She stuck out her tongue, wiggled her ears—this time her left one first, then her right—and turned the apples back into children.

"All right," said Maurecia, "let's go get Louis. He'll know what to do."

"No!" screamed Mrs. Gorf. "I'll turn you back into apples." She wiggled her ears—first her right one, then her left—and stuck out her tongue. But Jenny held up a mirror, and Mrs. Gorf turned herself into an apple.

The children didn't know what to do. They didn't have a teacher. Even though Mrs. Gorf was mean, they didn't think it was right to leave her as an apple. But none of them knew how to wiggle their ears.

Louis, the yard teacher, walked in. "Where's Mrs. Gorf?" he asked.

Nobody said a word.

"Boy, am I hungry," said Louis. "I don't think Mrs. Gorf would mind if I ate this apple. After all, she always has so many."

He picked up the apple, which was really Mrs. Gorf, shined it up on his shirt, and ate it.

Dear Me
Peter Ustinov

I had the choice, said my parents, who couldn't afford either, between St. Paul's and Westminster School. Students at the former wore straw hats, like Harold Lloyd; the latter, top hats like Fred Astaire. I thought that once I was to look ridiculous, I might as well look utterly ridiculous, and opted for Westminster. Officially I was not yet quite of a height to warrant a tailcoat, but since I was believed to be still growing, I was spared the ignominious bumfreezer reserved for smaller lads, a kind of black bolero with a collar spilling over the top like froth from a Guinness. As the greater of minute mercies I was given the clothes of an undertaker, together with a furled umbrella, in order, so the school brochure explained, to distinguish the boys from City of London Bank messengers. The final mockery on the head of a fourteen-year-old boy was a top hat, a crown of thorns if not a calvary, especially if your daily way to school took you through a virtual slum.

But there, for a year and a half, my parents wanted me both at home and away, the clearest indication of a love-hate relationship; and so I was sent away to school, not where my lungs might fill with ozone or my skin might burn in the wind, but a tuppenny bus ride from home. Of all possible compromises this was the most ludicrous and, for me, the most onerous. Far away I might have become used to new surroundings much more quickly, and reveled in a relative independence, become what they like to call a man, but this was frankly impossible in the shadow of Big Ben, with a bus stop just underneath the window of my dormitory, and my bus stopping there every five minutes.

Westminster is an exclusive school that has advanced rather happily with the times. It comprises both day boys and boarders and nestles in secrecy amid the ecclesiastical surroundings of what might be called the Kremlin of Westminster Abbey. There are arches galore on which to hit your head, steps of time-worn irregularity on which to break your neck, portraits of dead clerics before which to lose your faith. Owing to the proximity of Church House, the quiet bit of greenery known as Little Dean's Yard was invariably the striding ground of deans and bishops in couples, discussing some new posting or

administrative detail in terms of opulent secrecy.
And there was endless choir practice to rend the air,
some of the most appalling sharps and flats ever
emanating from the unbroken voices of unhappy
cherubim behind stained glass, evilly lit.

When all the boys were awaiting the daily morning prayers in the abbey, we looked like a migration
of crows which had made a haphazard landing in a
field. The pervading atmosphere was doggedly mo-
rose and gothic and our faces began to show the
premature signs of that nervous affectation which
passes for breeding. This impression was enhanced
by the fact that many sons of Members of Parlia-
ment were sent to Westminster, so that, whereas
their fathers were gripping their lapels in portentous
and jowly gravity a stone's throw away in the House
of Commons, the offspring were busy imitating their
fathers in school debates, waving notes instead of
order papers and bending their treble voices into all
the respectable mannerisms of British oratory.

"Indiah—" some piping voice would declare, and
pause, while its owner, stooped with a premature
bookishness, would scan the listeners for signs of
inattention—"Indiah" it would repeat, to drive
home a point which needed no driving—"Indiah
cannot be accorded home rule at this—ah—time."
And a groan of "Hear, hears" would rise from the
audience, punctuated by solitary bleats of "Shame"
from enlightened boy sopranos. I understood very
quickly the purpose of education such as this when I
was called aside by a master to tell me that I would
be involved in a debate, in order to second the

motion that "The Death Sentence Should Be Retained as a Deterrent." I informed the master in charge of debates that I was categorically opposed to the death sentence in all its forms, on moral grounds.

"That may be," said the master in a silky voice, "but you are still seconding the motion in favor of retention."

"I don't understand, sir—"

"You will," he chanted quietly and left.

I realized then that this was a school in which lawyers, diplomats, and businessmen were formed and there was no room here for the sloppy thinking of those who wished to change society.

I made what I deemed was an excellent speech against the death sentence, but such was the bloodthirsty temper of the times that there was an overwhelming vote in favor of retention, and my reputation as a debater rose in spite of what I had said. My eyes met those of the master. He was smiling slightly and nodded his congratulation at the victory of my side. I was being prepared for life, in more ways than one.

When new boys arrived, they were entertained at tea by the headmaster, who was at that time a clergyman of advanced age with a permanent grin of considerable intensity on his face. I have no doubt that the Very Reverend Dr. Costley-White was a good man, but he was also a big man, who walked quickly, so that the wind would make his black gown billow behind him, while the tassel on his mortarboard spread over his face like a claw. He frankly terrified new boys. When, during that initial tea party, he called out "Will no boy select the chocolate éclair?" there was no response, because no boy dared. "Oh very well," cried Dr. Costley-White and ate it himself.

After that benign and warmhearted introduction to my new school, my hopes rose, in spite of being what was known as a "fag" (not to be confused with the modern American usage of the word as a camp description of a homosexual; a fag in England was either a cigarette or else the nearest thing to a slave since William Wilberforce—a small boy at the beck and call of a big one). I was serving some kippers to the prefects in the medieval dining hall, which was one of the functions of fagging, when Dr. Costley-White swept into the room, his landing flaps down and his hat at a jaunty angle. His smile was spread from ear to ear as usual.

A pinup photo had been discovered, he bellowed, a pinup of a woman in a bathing costume, clutching a beach ball. He wished the perpetrator of this filth to own up at once. There was, of course, silence.

"Very well," he declared, as his smile attained even more extraordinary proportions, "When the culprit is found—and found, he will be—I shall beat him!" And then, very gently, as a summer breeze after a squall, "I am in the need of exercise."

As he turned to go, his gathering speed caused his grown to billow once again. I had the feeling he would take off as soon as he was out of sight.

Of course, what constitutes filth and the mysteries of sex have always been a cause of contention in

British schools. An old friend and mentor, Sir Clifford Norton, told me about sex education in Rugby before the First World War. The headmaster, who must have been an enlightened man, summoned all the boys who had reached the age of puberty to his study and, after reassuring himself that the door was firmly secured, made the following brief announcement: "If you touch it, it will fall off."

The boys were then invited to file back into their classes, now equipped to face adult life.

Many years later, Britain was still irked by this elusive yet fascinating subject. Arriving at a theater for a performance of a play of mine, I ran into a fellow actor of our troupe, Cyril Luckham, a true friend and magnificent performer who happens also to have very fair skin and hair. He gave every evidence of having wept. It is always disturbing when grown men are reduced to tears, so I took him aside and asked him tactfully what was the matter. He replied that nothing was the matter apart from laughter which had been racking him intermittently for the past couple of hours; and of course laughter and tears leave very similar aftereffects, especially in those of fair pigmentation.

He let me in on the cause of his joy. It was, apparently, the first day of a new term at his son's school. The headmaster, obeying the instructions of a government by now aware of the dangers of ignorance, was compelled to explain the facts of life to those of a certain age group. The poor man had been rehearsing his speech all through the summer recess, and eventually, in a panic of prudery, unable to bear the sniggers he could already hear in his head, he was reduced to composing a pamphlet, published at his own expense, which every boy found lying on his desk as the new term began.

This pamphlet began with the following seven words: "You may have noticed, between your legs . . ."

[My father] considered my reports from school a disgrace, he continued to harp on his own prowess as a scholar, and he called me lazy, which was undeniably true. I had foolishly gone on the modern side as opposed to the classical side in school, simply because two or three of my friends had taken that course, and now I was faced by mathematics, physics, and science on an unprecedented scale.

Of physics I could understand nothing at all. Why imaginary wheels should gather speed running down hypothetical slopes and create friction, I could neither understand in the terms in which it was taught, nor care about. As for chemistry, the acid smell of the lab made me queasy to start with and I was always distinctly nervous of spilling any substance smelling stronger than water on my fingers.

The master in charge of science was named F. O. M. Earp, from which his nickname of Fome, or Foam. He was a man so utterly dedicated to the abstractions of science that he would often point a finger between two boys and tell "that boy" to see him afterward. Since he never managed to aim at anyone in particular, nobody ever came to see him. By then he had forgotten the incident anyway. Once he mixed a couple of liquids in a test tube. There was a most resounding explosion, breaking several panes of glass in the lab. When the smoke cleared, there was no sign of Fome. He had disappeared, as in a fairy tale. There was an audible gasp from the boys, caught between shock and laughter. Then, slowly, he emerged from behind his desk, black, singed, and disheveled. "What did I do wrong, you!" he said in unemotional tones, pointing between me and my neighbor.

The whole classroom broke into a roar of relieved laughter.

Fome did not even smile.

"Come and see me afterwards, the boy responsible for the laughter."

Needless to say, I didn't, nor did my neighbor.

Owing to the shortage of teachers even then, Fome was supposed to teach not only chemistry but also divinity, of which he knew very little. He got around this difficulty, which might have daunted many less inventive spirits, especially in such unrelievedly ecclesiastical surroundings, by proceeding to explain most of Christ's miracles scientifically. It was clear from his attitude that even if he had mustered a little faith in Christ, he had absolutely none in the miracles. I do not remember in detail every one of his explanations, but do recollect him attributing the illusion of water turning into wine to the surreptitious addition of permanganate of potash, which could quite easily have bamboozled a crowd of simpletons.

In the field of sports, I had put my name down for tennis, the only sport for which I felt any real affinity, but my request was refused owing to a limited number of courts available, and I was made to row. This seemed to me a monotonous and draughty pursuit, and somehow wasteful to make all that effort in order to be going in the wrong direction. It is, in any case, never very reassuring for a young person of my weight to be seated in a boat seemingly made of cigar wrappers, and to be overlapping its sides.

I eventually took an inadvertent revenge on my tormentors during a "friendly" encounter with the second or third eight of another school. The old boy who had presented the school with the boat I was rowing in was bicycling along the riverside pathway bellowing incomprehensible instructions to us through a megaphone. He was in his sixties and affected the dress of a schoolboy in order to give us the garbled weight of his experience. Meanwhile the other school slipped gradually from view. At first I could see nine men out of the corner of my eye, then eight, then seven, then eventually nothing but a little disturbed water.

Then came an end to my misery. The fragile little seat beneath me was derailed and fell sideways. I immediately "caught a crab," and in attempting to resist the pressure of the water on my oar, I pushed the wheel of my seat through the hull. We began sinking, and there is no sight more ludicrous than eight men, with a small ninth the size of a jockey facing them, settling gracefully into the water in Indian file. The veteran on the shore, who had spent a lot of money on the boat, moaned, but since the sound of his distress was distorted by the mega-phone, he became as grotesque as everything else. We drifted helplessly into the side of a Dutch ship moored in the Thames, whose crew, far from help-ing us, bent over the rail and laid bets as to which of them could hit us squarely with gobs of spit. After that, miraculously, room was found for me on the tennis court. I learned yet another lesson.

I could at times beat members of the school tennis team in unofficial games, but I was only once on the team myself, and that was as a reserve. I came to the conclusion that there was something disconcerting about my personality as far as games masters were concerned, and that the undefinable quality which consistently got me out of trouble also kept me from being taken seriously as an athlete. Although I had inherited my mother's gifts as a sprinter, and had insufficient breath for the mile, and though my elevation and projection were entire-ly inadequate for jumps high or long, I was and—dare I say it?—even am surprisingly quick around the tennis court. In other words, when I see the point in moving quickly, I am capable of doing so.

. . . My morale was low not only due to frustra-tions, both at home and at school, but also to the ominous hurdle of examinations, called "O" levels today but called the School Certificate then, which plague youths in all countries and at all times. Rumors abounded then as they abound today. You couldn't even get a job as a dustman without one. In case of war, failure meant permanent relegation to the ranks. The majority of suicides in Japan were occasioned by a failure in exams. And so on and so forth.

There was little or no possibility of my passing them, at least on the modern side. Despite my prowess in certain subjects, I was absolutely without a vestige of hope in the general field of science and mathematics, and that was going to ruin my chances of advancement. At home, I hardly received any encouragement, although, to be fair, I doubt whether encouragement would have done much good.

My mother, who after all came from the Benois family as I have said, a clan that would have flinched had they thought for a moment that one of their scions was destined for the Stock Exchange, and would have suggested sculpture as a safer profession, now looked the facts squarely in the face. She recognized with a greater sense of reality than either Klop or I that I was not going to pass the School Certificate, and that it would cause the most terrible commotions in the household when the news of my failure was known. Why should I be put through this moral mangle, she argued, when I had no intention of being a chemist or a doctor or even a chartered accountant? Had I not held the attention of small audiences with my imitations? And what is the difference between small audiences and large ones except their size?

Before I left Westminster, there were mock elections in my house, encouraged by the headmaster under the guise of citizenship. We all made speeches and campaigned; and whereas it was natural in such a school that the Conservatives would win, there was a feeling of shock and even of dismay at the showing of the Liberals and Socialists, especially when we united in a kind of Front Populaire to form what was called the United Front of Progressive Forces, or Uffpuff. The headmaster met our delegation to reassure himself that we were neither subversive nor undemocratic in spirit, and when he found we were merely exasperated with the smugness of the Conservative majority, he blessed us with one of his more extravagant smiles.

I mention this with absolutely no wish to attribute any importance to our activities, but it is rather remarkable in retrospect that feelings ran high in one of the nobler seats of learning as early as 1937, and that the young were almost equally divided between unflinching support for the appeasement of Mr. Chamberlain and a desire to resist aggression before it was too late. There were those, young and inexperienced and foolish in many other ways, who were wise before the event.

I did not participate in many of the subsequent arguments, because I took an audition at Michel Saint-Denis's academy at Islington. Typically, I failed to understand the terms of the audition. One of the stipulations was to choose a page of any celebrated drama and learn it by heart. It did not occur to me that I was supposed to learn a single part, and that the other parts would be read by senior students, so I just took an arbitrary page of Shaw's *Saint Joan* and learned all the parts. My procedure seemed to amuse Michel Saint-Denis and George Devine, who was one of the other professors, and I was accepted even though they considered me, at sixteen, to be on the young side.

My mother begged them to take me, adding that, in her opinion, I had eyes very like M. Saint-Denis.

The great man studied me shamelessly through the swirling smoke of his pipe, and agreed.

"He has good eyes," he said in his French accent, and then added, with a sense of drama—"But, you realize, Nadia, that there will be divorce, there will be unpleasantness, there will be scandal, but *it must be like that!*"

His eyes lifted heavenward to await confirmation of his mystique, and I was launched into the world of adults, even if I was a little on the young side.

〰〰〰〰〰〰〰〰〰〰〰〰〰〰〰〰〰〰〰〰〰〰〰〰〰〰

Arithmetic
Carl Sandburg

〰〰〰〰〰〰〰〰〰〰〰〰〰〰〰〰〰〰〰〰〰〰〰〰〰〰

Arithmetic is where numbers fly like pigeons in and
out of your head.

Arithmetic tells you how many you lose or win if
you know how many you had before you lost or
won.

Arithmetic is seven eleven all good children go to
heaven—or five six bundle of sticks.

Arithmetic is numbers you squeeze from your head
to your hand to your pencil to your paper till you
get the answer.

Arithmetic is where the answer is right and everything is nice and you can look out of the window
and see the blue sky—or the answer is wrong and

you have to start all over and try again and see
how it comes out this time.

If you take a number and double it and double it
again and then double it a few more times, the
number gets bigger and bigger and goes higher
and higher and only arithmetic can tell you what
the number is when you decide to quit dou-
bling.

Arithmetic is where you have to multiply—and you
carry the multiplication table in your head and
hope you won't lose it.

If you have two animal crackers, one good and one
bad, and you eat one and a striped zebra with
streaks all over him eats the other, how many animal crackers will you have if somebody offers
you five six seven and you say No no no and you
say Nay nay nay and you say Nix nix nix?

If you ask your mother for one fried egg for break-
fast and she gives you two fried eggs and you
eat both of them, who is better in arithmetic, you
or your mother?

~~~~~~

Warning: Families May Be Dangerous
to Your Health
Erma Bombeck

~~~~~~

There's a lot of theories on why the American family is losing ground as an institution.

Some say it's economics . . . others say ecology . . . others blame lack of fulfillment . . . a few opt for priorities, or as one neighbor observed, "Would you want to bring a child into a world that wouldn't elect Ronald Reagan?"

I personally like the American family. It has a lot of potential. Besides, the world is not geared for two people. Twinkies come twelve to a box, kitchen chairs, four to a set, gum, five sticks to the package.

To my way of thinking, the American family

started to decline when parents began to communicate with their children. When we began to "rap," "feed into one another," "let things hang out" that mother didn't know about and would rather not.

Foremost of the villains that ripped the American family to shreds was Education. It was a case of Hide-and-Seek meeting Show and Tell . . . the McGuffey reader crowd locking horns with the Henry Miller group.

The ignorance gap that the new math created between parent and child has not even begun to mend.

Before the new math, I had a mysterious aura about me. I never said anything, but my children were convinced I had invented fire.

When we began to have "input" with one another, my daughter said to me one day, "Mama, what's a variable?"

"It's a weirdo who hangs around the playground. Where did you read that word? On a restroom wall?"

"It's in my new math book," she said. "I was hoping you could help me. They want me to locate the mantissa in the body of the table and determine the associated antilog ten, and write the characteristics as an exponent on the base of ten."

I thought a minute. "How long has the mantissa been missing?"

She went to her room, locked her door and I never saw her again until after she graduated.

The metric system was no better. Once a child knows that a square millimeter is .00155 square inches, will he ever have respect for a mother who once measured the bathroom for carpeting and found out she had enough left over to slipcover New Jersey?

And what modern-day mother has never been intimidated when she has to communicate with a child's teacher?

I don't think there's anything that makes my morning like a kid looking up from his cereal and saying casually, "I gotta have a note saying I was sick or my teacher won't let me back into school."

"I suppose it has to be written on paper," I ask, slumping miserably over the bologna.

"The one you wrote on wax paper she couldn't read. But if you can't find paper, I could stay home for another day," he said.

I tore a piece of wallpaper off the wall and said, "Get me a pencil."

The pencil took a bit of doing. After a fifteen-minute search we finally found a stub in the lint trap of the dryer.

"You sure are whipped up about this note," I sighed.

"You don't understand," he said. "If we don't have one we don't go back to school."

I started to write. "Is your teacher a Miss, a Ms. or a Mrs.?"

"I don't know," he pondered. "She owns her own car and carries her own books."

"Dear Ms. Weems," I wrote.

"On the other hand, she stayed up to watch the Miss America Pageant."

"Dear Miss Weems," I wrote.

"It doesn't matter," he shrugged. "When she has her baby we'll have a new teacher."

"Dear MRS. Weems," I wrote. "Please excuse Brucie from school yesterday. When he awoke in the morning he complained of stomach cramps and . . ."

"Cross out stomach cramps," he ordered, "tell her I was too sick to watch TV."

"Dear Mrs. Weems, Brucie had the urgencies and . . ."

"What does urgencies mean?"

"Stomach cramps."

"Don't tell her that! The last time you wrote that she put me next to the door and didn't take her eyes off me all day long."

"It was your imagination," I said. "Do you need a note or not?"

"I told you I can't go to school without it."

"Okay then, get me the dictionary and turn to the D's."

He looked over my shoulder. "What does D-I-A-R-R-H-E-A mean?"

"It means you sit by the door again," I said, licking the envelope.

Composing the note took twenty-five minutes, which was eight minutes longer than the signing of the Declaration of Independence. I wouldn't bring it up, but only yesterday I was cleaning out a jacket pocket and there was the note: unread and unnecessary.

To me, modern education is a contradiction. It's like a three-year-old kid with a computer in his hand who can multiply 10.6 percent interest of $11,653, but doesn't know if a dime is larger or smaller than a nickel.

It is like your daughter going to college and taking all your small appliances, linens, beddings, furniture, luggage, TV set and car and then saying, "I've got to get away from your shallow materialism."

My kids always talk a great game of ecology. Yet, they harbor the No. 1 cause of pollution in this country: gym clothes.

A pair of shorts, a shirt and a pair of gym shoes walked into the utility room under their own steam last Wednesday and leaned helplessly against the wall. I stood there while I watched a pot of ivy shrivel and die before my eyes.

Blinking back the tears, I yelled to my son, "How long has it been since these clothes have been washed?"

"Since the beginning of the school year," he shouted back.

"What school year?"

"1972–1973."

"I thought so. You know, I don't know how your P.E. teacher stands it."

"He said we weren't too bad until yesterday."

"What happened yesterday?"

"It rained and we came inside."

"Don't you have rules about laundering these things?"

"Yeah. We have to have them washed every four months whether they need it or not."

Carefully, I unfolded the muddy shorts, the brittle T-shirt and the socks that were already in the final stages of rigor mortis.

As I tried to scrape off a French fry entangled in a gym shoestring, I couldn't help but reflect that this was a child who had been reared in an antiseptic world. When he was a baby, I used to boil his toys and sterilize his navel bands. I made the dog wear a mask when he was in the same room. I washed my hands BEFORE I changed his diapers.

Where had I failed?

Under his bed were dirty clothes that were harboring wildlife. In his drawers were pairs of soiled underwear so old that some had plastic liners in them. His closet had overalls and jeans that hung suspended without the need of hangers.

Opening the lid of the washer, I felt around trying to find the gym clothes that I had just washed. I retrieved a shoestring, two labels and a clean French fry.

"What happened to my gym clothes?" asked my son.

"After the sweat and dirt went, this was all that was left."

Probably the most blatant contradiction between what a child is at home and what he is at school manifests itself at the annual Athletic Banquet.

Next time you attend an athletic awards banquet, catch the look on the faces of mothers as the accomplishments of their sons and daughters are revealed. It is as if they are talking about a different person with the same name as your youngster.

By intense concentration, you can sometimes read the parents' thoughts, as the coaches pay them homage.

"Mark is probably one of the best sprinters I've had in my entire career here at So. High. Hang onto your hats, people. Mark ran the hundred-yard dash in nine point nine!"

(Had to be nine days and nine hours. I once asked him to run out the garbage and it sat by the sink until it turned into a bookend.)

"I don't know what the baseball team would do without Charlie. We've had chatterers on the team before who get the guys whipped up, but Charlie is the all-time chatterer. There isn't a moment when he isn't saying something to spark the team."

(Charlie speaks six words to me in a week. "When you going to the store?")

"For those of you who don't really understand field events, I want to explain about the shotput. It's a ball weighing eight pounds that was thrown a hundred feet by an outstanding athlete here at So. . . . Wesley Whip."

(That's funny. Wesley looks like the same boy who delivers my paper and can't heave a six-ounce Saturday edition all the way from his bike to my porch.)

"Wolf Man Gus will go down in football annals

as one of the all-time greats here at So. High. In the game with Central, Gus scored the winning touchdown despite a chipped bone in his ankle, a dislocated shoulder and a fever of a hundred and two."

(So how come Wolf Man Gus stays home from school every time he has his teeth cleaned?)

"I don't suppose anyone has better reflexes in this entire state than our outstanding basketball rebounder, Tim Rim. When the Good Lord passed out coordination, Tim was first in line."

(Tim is seventeen years old and I can still only pour him a half-glass of milk because that's all I want to clean up.)

"Tennis is a gentleman's game. This year's recipient of the Court Courtesy award is none other than So. High's Goodwill Ambassador, Stevie Cool."

(He's certainly come a long way since he tried to break his brother's face last week when he took a record album without asking.)

"The swimming team would never have made it this year without our plucky little manager, Paul Franswarth. Paul picks up those wet towels off the floor, hangs up the suits to dry, and is responsible for putting all the gear back where it belongs."

(Let's go home, Ed. I feel sick.)

Snowflaketime
Jean Kerr

I've been hearing that overproduction and high costs are killing the theater, but I don't know that I actually worried about such things until I saw *Snowflaketime,* the third-grade Christmas play at a school in Larchmont. Then it all came clear to me.

Here was a dazzling production with a chorus of sixty angels in pink gauze, who sang "The First Noel" three times. There was, in addition, a chorus of sixty angels in white gauze, who handed tinsel stars to the angels in pink gauze. There were twenty toy soldiers in red felt uniforms with gold rifles, of whom nineteen were able to march backward. There were 120 dancers "from every land" but mostly from the Balkan countries. There were two scarecrows who had taken tap-dancing and twelve jack-in-the-boxes.

Oh, the whole thing was a "triumph," "a visual delight," and a "stunning success." But of course it will never pay off. Even with a thirty-five-cent top and a capacity house (the house seats six hundred, with each mother seating one or two extra depending on the width of the mother), they're going to have trouble getting their money back.

Our eight-year-old, who was wrapped in tissue paper and red ribbons and was supposed to be a present, was very distressed because two of the toy soldiers waved at the audience. As my husband remarked, that's the kind of thing they would have cleaned up if they had taken the show to New Rochelle for a couple of weeks. But I imagine they were afraid of those out-of-town losses.

When I was in third grade we didn't gear our productions to the tired business boy. We eschewed extravaganzas. Well, it wasn't so much that we eschewed them; we'd never heard of them. We did the "great" plays—*Nahaliel, The Shepherd, The Shepherd's Gift,* and *The Young Shepherd Boy.* We did them on a shoestring, but with the sense of doom and dedication of some movie actors doing a revival of Ibsen.

I always played the tallest shepherd. I wore my father's old dressing gown and I said, "Full many a moon have I watched on yon hill, and ne'er saw I such a star as this." In an effort to suggest great age, I used to make my voice creak and crackle like a short-wave receiver. All the shepherds were very, very old (the mystery is how they were ever able to watch any sheep), except for one shepherd boy whose characterization changed from year to year.

Sometimes he brought his flute, his only possession, and laid it in the manger. Other years he was lame and brought his crutch. He never came empty-handed and he always had a big scene in which he sobbed and said, "I, Nahaliel, have naught, naught save only this flute (or crook or crutch or whatever it was that year), but freely do I give it to THEE." Then he threw himself down in the straw.

There was a part for an actress. I finally did play Nahaliel, but I started at the bottom. Actually, the first thing I played was part of the scenery. No one was allowed to nail anything to our stage floor, so all the scenery had to be held up by the students. On this occasion I stood behind a large balsam tree and with my free hand shook Lux flakes on Mary and Joseph as they passed, the while making low humming sounds to indicate the inclement state of the weather. My family regarded this triple accomplishment with mixed emotions. As a matter of fact, I don't think my father's were too mixed. I recall his inquiring bleakly, as the evening of my debut approached, "My God, do you mean we're going to have to get dressed and go all the way up there to see her stand behind a tree?"

Our audiences, generally, came prepared for a profound emotional experience, which may explain why certain locations, directly behind pillars, were in great demand. We always had standees at the rear of the house, even when the auditorium was half empty. But we were proud, and the overhead was low.

Nowadays you hardly see a shepherd at all. As far as the school in Larchmont is concerned, I sensed a shift away from the serious theater even before Christmas. Some weeks ago our oldest boy came home with the information that he was appearing in a Safety Play. His costume was to be very simple. He was playing a back tire. I asked him what his part consisted of, and he said, "Oh, mostly I just blow out." What I want to know is, will this equip him to play the great parts like Lear or even a front tire? At that, I can scarcely wait for him to play Lear. It'll be so much easier to make the costume.

I suppose that, for the untalented, all costumes are hard. John (age four) came home recently with a yellow slip pinned to his sleeve announcing that his nursery school was going to present *Frosty, the Snowman,* and John was playing—oh, the wonder of it! and why wasn't there a phone call from *Variety*—Frosty.

"You can make the costume out of a worn sheet and an old top hat from the attic," wrote his teacher. The note concluded with the inexplicable statement: "In the first scene Frosty is supposed to be half melted." (Why tell me? As I explained to Johnny, it's the actor's job to characterize. I just make costumes.)

Johnny plowed upstairs ahead of me to find an old sheet in the linen closet, and the next thing I heard was a sob of anguish. "Mommy"—it was the cry of Oedipus on the heights of Colonus—"our sheets are GREEN!" And so they were. In a burst of whimsy some years ago I had purchased all colored sheets. When I think of those Pepperell people, so full of loud talk about the myriad wonders that can be wrought with colored sheets! I'd like to see them try to make a snowman costume sometime.

But never mind the sheet. What old top hat? What attic? We don't keep old top hats in our attic. We keep academic gowns, white Palm Beach suits that are bound to come back in style, and three storm windows that evidently belong to another house.

When it came right down to it, though, there was nothing to making that costume. By giving up lunch I whipped the whole thing up in less than a month. And finally the day arrived. Johnny was a superb Frosty. His was an exquisitely conceived, finely wrought performance—limpid, luminous, tender. When he took his bows there was tremendous applause, in which he enthusiastically joined. I could just hear him in Congress, forty years from now, referring to himself as "the able senator from New York."

This production ended, however, in a short tableau that said to me that the day of economy and sincerity was not wholly past. A small red-headed boy in a brown toga, with dirty sneakers showing briefly beneath, escorted a tiny girl in white dress and blue veil across the stage. He stopped suddenly and said, in a voice of piercing sweetness:

"Oh, Mary, 'tis a cold, cold night."

Mary turned and said simply, " 'Tis."

It won't make a nickel, but it's a great audience show.

Teachers
Sam Levenson

Not to be outdone by Pickle Week, Foot Care
Week and Remember the Buffalo Week, some
teachers' organizations have managed to promote a
Teachers' Recognition Day. My parents did not
need to be prodded by public-relations programs
into an attitude of respect for teachers. I was raised
to believe that teachers were infallible and super-
human. A teacher was not like a relative, a neighbor, or even a friend. When a teacher passed on the
street the mothers stopped whatever they were doing
and bowed their heads slightly in acknowledgment
of her presence. The fathers, who rarely tipped their
hats to anyone, did so in respectful silence to a

teacher. She was above parents and just a little below God, and as such was held in the kind of awe that bordered on fear.

As a child I could never conceive of a teacher's being subject to the habits of ordinary people. We never saw her eat, or drink, or scratch, or blow her nose, or, perish the thought, go to the bathroom. Her conduct was as stainless as her stiffly starched blouse.

If there was an occasional parents' meeting in the evening Mama went, only to doze off during the principal's speech. She didn't have to listen. The principal was an educated person, and educated people could do no wrong. "She knows what she's talking about." That was good enough for Mama.

The attitude of the teacher toward the parent was that of a professional toward an amateur. She would not think of asking the parent's advice any more than a doctor would ask his patient for a prescription. As far as the children were concerned, any sign of resistance to her hegemony over their minds and bodies was deemed a mutiny and dealt with accordingly.

A "B" in conduct was the equivalent of a scarlet letter. It meant I had offended God, man, and country. I was guilty of high treason. Mama would wring her hands in grief: "What have we come to? Look at me, bum, son of Cain, thug. Better to look at me than at a judge." Brother Joe joined in, "Whatsamatta? You a wise guy or something?" And brother Jack: "Making trouble for the teacher? Pa-

pa works all day in the shop so you can be a hoodlum or something?" And Mike: "Swear on your pinkie you'll never be bad again."

I was bad again. This time it was a matter of lateness. My teacher told me I would have to bring my mother. In those days "Bring your mother" were the most frightening words a teacher could say to a child.

I was trapped in a no-man's land. Mama had said "If I have to go to school for you once more, don't come home from school" on the very same day that the teacher had said "Don't come back without your mother."

I appealed to the candy-store lady near the school. I explained that my mother was sick and couldn't come to school, and would she please act as my mother, for which my own mother would be eternally grateful. She came and listened to the list of charges against me read aloud by the teacher before the entire class. Mrs. Candy Store got carried away by her role and outdid my own mother. She turned to me in a rage:

"Is this true, all that the nice teacher is saying about you?"

Without looking up I answered, "Yes."

The stand-in then gave me a clout on the head like I had never gotten from my own mother.

I was late once more. At this point in my life, crime set in. I played hooky.

Experienced hooky players know what to do with their ill-gained time. I didn't. The hours weighed heavily on my hands. I realized that I had better get out of my own neighborhood. I walked for miles. It wasn't easy to find a neighborhood in which there were no mothers. I felt that all eyes were turned on me. "That's him!" I avoided all men in uniform: policemen, firemen, street cleaners, mailmen, Western Union messengers and milkmen.

I had no money and I was starved. Maybe I ought to run away from home, get a job in Bridgeport, become very successful and then send for the whole family who would then forgive me in my mansion. How old did you have to be to join the Navy? I saw kids from other schools going home for lunch and then going back to school, some with a cooky in the hand. Lucky kids, they had mothers. I had disowned mine by playing hooky. Maybe Mama would die because of me. I timed my arrival home at exactly ten past three. My bread-and-butter was waiting for me as usual. Thank God, Mama was no truant.

The next morning I found out that crime doesn't pay. My classmates greeted me with: "Where were you yesterday? We had a great time. The teacher was absent."

The worst offense in class was to break the silence. Classrooms today are built with acoustical tile to soundproof the room. In those days they soundproofed us. There was comfort in knowing that no matter how many times you changed schools you could never fall very far behind. Punishments were uniform. You had a choice of standing in the corner facing the wall ("That will teach you a lesson");

writing "Columbus discovered America in 1492" five hundred times; staying after school and washing the blackboards (causing in the habitual mischief-maker a chronic case of dishpan hands); putting out your hand for a rap on the knuckles; being kept after school with your hands clasped on the desk till death (or teacher) do us part; or, in severe cases, being demoted an entire grade, where the work, at least, was familiar. There was no point in complaining to Mama about all this because she would only say, "That will teach you a lesson."

When the opportunity presented itself we were not long in rebelling against the strict discipline. Those were memorable times—especially the day the teacher said, "I have to go to the principal's office for a few moments. I trust that you will behave like ladies and gentlemen while I'm gone. Arthur will take charge until I return and will report any misbehavior."

Stoolpigeon Arthur, up there all alone silhouetted against the blackboard, made a beautiful target. A blackboard eraser made a perfect landing on his head and blinded him with a burst of powdered chalk. That was the signal. All inhibitions were wiped out in a sudden explosion of pent-up energy. From each according to his ability. The artists went to work drawing pictures of the teacher on all the blackboards. The air force sent out paper gliders in mass formation. The fire fighters splashed ink in all directions. One kid took the teacher's pitch pipe out of her desk and tore off a hot "Tiger Rag" while the boys paired off in couples to dance on the desks.

The rhythm was supplied by the percussion division pulling on the window-shade cords. In the background could be heard the muffled cries of six girls who had been locked into the coat closet.

"Hey, Nelson! You be teacher." Nelson stuffed his shirt with paper to simulate the female form, made his rear end protrude abnormally, banged his ruler on the desk and shouted, "Clahss! We shahl hahve a two minute drrill! Breathe in! Breathe out! Knee bending! Ahll togethah. Down! Up! Down! Up!"

"Hey, fellers, she's coming," cried the lookout. It took about one millionth of a second for us to quiet down. You could hear the air humming. Gray-haired Arthur took over again and life went back to normal.

Our teacher's announcement that we were going to have an assembly was always greeted with joyous excitement. Give us anything but arithmetic.

We were paraded into the auditorium. A short and plump teacher played a march on an immense piano that looked like a mahogany coffin with keys, while a tall and skinny teacher stood on the stage clapping her hands rhythmically, calling out, "Left, right, left, right." We would come down the center aisle, then separate—boys to the right, girls to the left—and wait at our seats while the color guard stumbled onto the stage. Then came "The Star-Spangled Banner," always followed by "Your singing today is very disappointing, children." We could not sit down until the tall teacher signaled with her long ruler. We came down with a crash and a burst of talking. "Class stand. That was very poorly done. Your sitting is very disappointing today. We shall practice sitting down until you can do it like ladies and gentlemen. Ready!" Signal. "Sit! That boy in the back, see me after class. Stand! Sit! Stand! Sit! Stand! Stand! Sit!"

The principal, hoping to uplift us, would mumble a verse from the Bible, one that I have never been able to locate since—something about not smiting the Smithsonians lest thee thyself be smooten.

Without interruption she would then continue with "We have several important announcements to make. Classes 3B-2, 5B-1, 6B-3, 7B-4, 8B-1, 4B-5, 1A-6, 6A-1 and Ungraded 1 have all achieved one hundred per cent G.O. membership." (Applause.) "The Archery Club will practice in the lunchroom today during the lunch period."

The tall teacher took over again. "That will be all for today. Let us make our exit an improvement over our entrance. Class stand! Class sit! Try it again. Class stand! Girls will face right, boys will face left. Those near the windows will face right, those near the front will face back, those near the back will face front. Forward march!" We all marched forward into each other. We were kept after school for an hour to practice exiting like ladies and gentlemen.

How to Behave at School
Delia Ephron

Ma, I don't feel good. Maybe I shouldn't get up today. I feel sorta blah. I don't know—I just feel yucky all over. Ma? Ma, would you feel my forehead? I don't? Are you sure? Are you positive? OK, I'll get up. I'll get up, but you'll see—I'll probably just get to school and have to turn around and come home again.

Arrive at school late. Explain that you are tardy because you couldn't find your shoe.

As soon as the teacher turns to write on the blackboard, open your desk, pull out *Mad* magazine, and put it inside the language arts workbook. Read *Mad* magazine while it looks as if you are reading language arts.

71

Chew a pencil, tear off the corner of a piece of paper, and write: "You are a dodo. Pass it on." Gripping the pencil between your teeth like a pirate with a knife in his mouth, fold note in half, quarters, eighths. Use your ear as a pencil holder as you drop the note on the floor and pass it with your foot to your friend across the aisle. Then, pretending to play the drums, tap your desk with a pencil, and when it's time to hit the cymbals, tap the head of the kid in front. If he turns around and says, "Cut it out," say, "Cut *what* out?" As soon as he faces front again, kick him and say, "Sorry, I didn't mean to." Click your pen.

Deny that you are chewing gum and stick it on the roof of your mouth.

Whisper. Stop when the teacher asks if you'd prefer to spend class in the hall. Ask to change your seat.

Pretend that your pencils are ships; steer them around your desk and make them collide. Look at the clock.

When the teacher asks for a volunteer to take names while she is out of the classroom, raise your hand, shake it frantically, stretch so that your body is nearly a horizontal line between your desk and the teacher, and call out, "Me, me, me, me, me, me, me." You do not get chosen.

What to do While the Teacher Is Out of the Classroom: Hold your nose and say in a high-pitched voice, "Now class, behave." Run to the front of the room and draw your fingernails down the blackboard. Return to your seat like Groucho Marx, hunched over, looking both ways, wiggling eyebrows, and chomping on a pencil as if it were a cigar. Get your name taken.

Get it erased by threatening to get the name-taker at recess.

Sail a paper airplane and when it lands, raise your hands, clasp them above one shoulder, then the other: You are the champ. Get your name taken.

Throw an eraser.

When a kid shoots a spitball and doesn't get his name taken, say, "How come you took my name and not his?" Get his name taken while he tells you to shut up, calls you by your last name only, and says, "Mind your own beeswax." Burp.

Smell something funny. Shriek, "Someone laid one, someone laid one, silent-but-deadly, smell-y, whew, P.U., major fart alert, major fart alert, major fart alert." Wave hand in front of face. Crack up. Pound desk. Hold nose while each kid in the class also holds his nose and insists that it was another kid.

Yell, "She's coming," and fall out of your chair just as the teacher returns.

Ask to get something from your coat in the cloakroom.

Ask to sharpen your pencil.

Tell the teacher, for the second time this week, that you do not have your homework because the dog ate it. She will say that if this kind of behavior continues, she will have to note it on your permanent record card.

Look at the clock.

Ask to get a drink of water.

In the Hall

Look in all the classrooms you pass, stopping at one or two long enough to attract attention and distract the students—stick thumbs in ears and wave fingers, or scratch armpits like a monkey and heave up and down. If a class has its door closed, jump up to see through the window on the door. Play hopscotch, using floor tiles as squares. Stand against the wall and inch your way down the hall —you are in a spy movie. When you reach a corner, peek around it. After turning up the water at the fountain to see how high it will go, fill up your squirt gun. Walk back to class with the point of the gun in your mouth; keep pulling the trigger.

As soon as you return, check the clock to see how much time you killed.

How to Act if You Do Not Want to Be Called on

• Make yourself invisible. Align head and shoulders with those of a student directly between the teacher and you. If the teacher moves, adjust alignment.

• Make yourself inconspicuous. To accomplish this, assume a casual pose. Concentrate on fitting the top of the pen into the bottom; perhaps even hum to yourself. Or engage in nonchalant play with a pencil: Hold it upright, point against paper, and slide fingers from eraser to tip. Turn pencil over; slide from tip to eraser. Turn and slide. Turn and slide.

If the teacher calls on you anyway, do not respond immediately in the hope that a kid with the answer will just yell it out. If no one rescues you and the question calls for a yes or no response, pick one. Otherwise, give a joke answer. The class will laugh. The teacher will say that it won't be so funny when you get your report card.

At Recess

With tongue, remove gum from roof of mouth and continue chewing.

Stand around. Discuss bedtimes. Say that you stayed up until midnight to finish your homework. Your friend will answer, that's nothing, he stayed up until two o'clock, and you can respond, "Big deal, last week I was up until four." Add that on weekends you can stay up as late as you want, once you were up all night, and has he ever been to a drive-in movie? Your dad took you. Show each other your fillings. Announce whether you are a Democrat or a Republican and take a position on the coming election based on your parents' conversation the night before. Discuss Hydrox versus Oreo. Compare chunky peanut butter and creamy. Argue about the most sickening vegetable. Compare number of rooms in your house, counting closets. Compare allowances. Choose whether you would rather freeze to death or be burned alive. Feel each other's mus-

cles. Say that you got a break on your new car
'cause your dad knows the dealer. Say that your dad
thinks foreign cars are better. Say that he likes "four
on the floor." Discuss brands of sneakers. Try to
step on each other's shoes. Demonstrate how to
make a fart noise by putting your hand in your
armpit and squeezing. Say that you know the
longest word in the English language—antidisestab-
lishmentarianism. Bet that no one can spell it.

Walk around wearing wax mustaches and red
lips.

See if M&Ms will melt in your hand.

Eat red-hots and show off your red tongue.

Promise that you'll be a kid's best friend if he
gives you a Tootsie Pop. Wish that you would hurry
up and get to the center of it while you listen to a
riddle: Why did the little moron take a ladder to the
party? Because he heard that drinks were on the
house.

Say, "Guess what?" When a kid says, "What?"
say, "That's what." Do it again and again until you
come to a kid who, when you say, "Guess what?"
says, "That's what."

There is a student whose head is kind of flat on
top. Skip around the playground chanting, "Flathead, flathead, flathead."

To be immune from a kid with cooties, give
yourself a cootie shot.

Put your finger over the spout of the drinking
fountain to direct the spray so it hits everyone.
When the water soaks a kid's pants, shriek that
everyone will think he wet them. Hold the faucet

handle for a friend to take a drink and, when he leans over, let the water die down. Say, "OK, OK, I'll do it right. Honest. Word of honor. Trust me. Really, don't worry," and when he leans down again, turn it up full force. Take a drink, hold water in mouth, chase a kid and spray him. Do it again, but this time burst out laughing before you get a chance at a good shot. While screaming, repeat all water activities until the playground supervisor threatens to bench you.

Stand under the jungle gym and look under girls' skirts. Tell a girl that you'll give her a nickel if she'll climb up.

Lie on the ground just in case a girl walks by.

Ask a girl in a dress to stand on her head.

Listen to a kid tell a dirty joke. Laugh hysterically. Do not have any idea what you are laughing at.

Envy the kid with a broken leg. Beg for a turn on his crutches.

Pretend that you do not know your little sister.

Be chased by girls.

When a boy falls off the jungle gym and gets his front teeth knocked out, yell, "I'll do it, I'll do it, I'll do it," collect the pieces, and turn them into the nurse's office. Even though the nurse's office smells funny, hang around to try to get a look at the boy.

Play tag. Argue about whether you were touched. Play war. Argue about whether you were killed. Play kickball. Argue about whether you were out. Play dodge ball. Argue about whether you were hit. Play statues. Argue about whether you moved. Take sides when everyone else argues. If necessary, scream about fairness and call the other side names, such as jerks, creeps, crumbs, liars, and dirty cheaters.

Get benched. On your way there, think that it's not fair. Think that the kid you hit, who hit you back and you hit again, will be sorry. Think that you'll get him, that you'll never speak to him again, never walk to school with him again, invite him to your house or birthday party. Think, "Just let him come within ten feet of me."

After sitting on the bench for a minute, see how far you can stand from the bench and still be considered benched. Stick your gum under the bench.

In the Boys' Lavatory

Aim at the side of the toilet. Do not flush.

At Assembly

"I pledge allegiance to the flag of the United States of America. And to the Republic for Richard stands, one nation, under God, indivisible, with liberty and justice for all." Sit down.

Crane neck around to see where teacher is sitting.

As the film on fire prevention—starring Otto, the talking car—begins, take a marble out of your pocket and roll it between your hands. Putting hand up to mouth as if to stifle a yawn, pop the marble in. With your tongue, shove it over to your cheek so that it sticks out and makes a lump. Push it with your tongue over to your other cheek. See how fast you can move it from one cheek to another. Take it out. Clench it in your eye like a monocle. Stuff it in your nose. Leave it there—half in, half out—then poke your best friend. He shouldn't miss it.

Listen to the kid at the end of the row crack his knuckles. Listen to the kid next to him crack his knuckles. Listen to the third kid crack his knuckles. Listen to the fourth kid. Crack your knuckles. Listen to the kid after you.

Fight over the armrest.

Look at the projector to see how much film is left.

Drop your marble.

As soon as the projector breaks, start whispering. Stop when the teacher snaps her fingers, but do not look at her. She might point at you and then stick her thumb over her shoulder: Out! Try to get the attention of your girl friend by enlarging yourself somewhat: Clasp hands behind head and rise up, stretching.

Watch the kid fix the projector. Wish that you were a member of the AV squad.

As soon as the film resumes, fall asleep.

"The assembly is now adjourned. Will the classes please leave quietly, passing out of the auditorium front rows to back."

Walking Home

Step on a crack, break your mother's back. Take it one step per pavement square. *Step on a line, break your mother's spine*. Two steps per pavement square. Skip every other square. Pull leaves off hedges. Kick a rock as you walk. Avoid quicksand. Be your own horse: Say "Giddyup," and slap your thigh. Jump up; grab a branch of a tree. Run—you are being chased by red ants. Ring the bell, hit the knocker, slam the door, shout, "Hey Mom, it's me," and race to the bathroom.

"How was school?"

"Fine."

"What's new?"

"Nothing."

"What did you do today?"

"I don't know—the usual."

Then add, "I'm starved," and on your way to the kitchen, tell your mom the riddle: Why did the little moron take a ladder to the party? Because he heard that drinks were on the roof.

TEEN POWER

The Mad Shakespeare Primer
Mad Magazine

No Holds Bard Dept.

"Why don't kids read the classics anymore?" MAD submitted this question to ten of our top Educators in order to find out. Unfortunately, nine of them ignored us completely. However, the tenth submitted a 14 page treatise that probed deeply into the reasons. But we couldn't understand all them big words he used, so we decided to answer our own questions outselves: the reason kids don't read the classics anymore is because they're not properly introduced to them at an early age. Why not start youngsters off with simplified versions of the classics, like f'rinstance these, in . . .

THE MAD SHAKESPEARE PRIMER

Romeo and Juliet
Lesson 1.

See the teenager.
His name is Romeo.
He is climbing Juliet's trellis.
Climb, climb, climb.
Why is Romeo climbing Juliet's trellis?
That's how teenagers smooched in those days.
Which explains the gym bloomers.
After all, you can't go around climbing trellises
    in your street clothes.
Today, Romeo would use the stairs.
Or better still, park out front and honk.
Honk, honk, honk.
He certainly wouldn't climb Juliet's trellis.
He'd be arrested as a juvenile delinquent.

Romeo and Juliet
Lesson 2.

This is Juliet.
She wants to marry Romeo.
Silly gym bloomers and all.
Which explains the dunce cap.
But Juliet's daddy has forbidden the marriage.
Forbid, forbid, forbid.
This has made Juliet very sad.
She has been very quiet ever since.
Quiet, quiet, quiet.
Juliet has always been a quiet girl.
But not *this* quiet.
Why is Juliet so quiet?

Because she has committed suicide.
Too bad, Juliet.
You should have been born 400 years later.
Then you could have gotten married.
LIFE Magazine would have helped you elope!

Macbeth
Lesson 1.

See the witches stir.
Stir, stir, stir.
What are the witches stirring?
They are stirring up trouble.
The trouble is for Macbeth.
Surprise, Macbeth!
The witches tell Macbeth he will be King.
Macbeth does not want to be King.
Macbeth just wants to be Thane of Cawdor.
Whatever-in-heck that is!
But Mrs. Macbeth wants him to be King.
Wants, wants, wants.
You know the type.
Pushy!

Macbeth
Lesson 2.

See the lady.
She is Mrs. Macbeth.
She is washing her hands.
Because her hands are all bloodstained.
Ecch, ecch, ecch!
She has just helped Macbeth kill the King.
Why did Mrs. Macbeth help Macbeth kill the
King?

Because the Macbeths always do everything
    together!
Togetherness, togetherness, togetherness.
"Out, damned spot!" says Mrs. Macbeth.
Mrs. Macbeth has dirty hands, all right.
She also has a dirty mouth!

Hamlet
Lesson 1.

See the man.
His name is "Hamlet."
He is the hero of the play.
The play is named after him.
It is called "Hamlet."
That figures!
It is lucky Hamlet has such an elegant name.
Can you imagine a Shakespeare play named
    "Rock"?
Or "Tab"?
Hamlet says, "Something is rotten in the State
    of Denmark!"
Rotten, rotten, rotten.
That also figures.
They didn't have deep frezers in those days!

Hamlet
Lesson 2.

"Hamlet" is a very interesting play.
It contains stuff to make you think.
Think, think, think.
It also contains:
Two knifings,

Three fatal duels,
Two suicides,
One poisoning,
And a double execution.
"Hamlet" is a good play for children.
It is much better than watching violent TV
    programs.
It is much better than reading violent comic
    books.
Because it is more violent than TV and comic
    books put together!

Julius Caesar
Lesson 1.

See the mighty Caesar.
See Julius, the conquering General!
See Caesar, the invincible Emperor!
See, see, see!
Better look quick, though.
This may be your last chance.
Tomorrow, Caesar will be dead as a mackerel.
Some of the Senators will stab him in the Forum.

Also in the Duodenum, Esophagus, and Belly.
Stab, stab, stab.
Tough bananas, Julius.
That's what you get for going into politics!

Julius Caesar
Lesson 2.

See Julius's friend, Marc Antony.
Marc Anthony is running for Emperor now.

He is making a speech at Julius's funeral.

Which can be even more sickening than kissing babies.

When Marc Antony wins, he and his friends will have orgies.

Whee, whee, whee!

They will eat candied humming birds' wings.

Yum, yum, smack!

And drink lots of wine.

Glugg, glugg, hic!

And after dinner, they'll throw people to the lions.

Growl, growl, urrp!

People really knew how to live in those days!

Offsides

Andrew Ward

My height might have afforded a natural athlete some magnificent opportunities, but my growth rate always seemed to me ominous, like the overextension of a rubber band. In the mirror at night I would examine with growing alarm the stretch marks which cross-hatched my middle like tribal tattoos, and I had a nightmare once in which I actually split apart and had to be patched together with special elastic substances. My bedroom was a half-refurbished cellar rec area in a home of niggardly construction. The acoustical-tiled ceiling was six feet high, and I was always parting my hair on the halo-shaped fluorescent light fixtures in the dark.

I was nearing my present height of six feet four inches by the tenth grade, and had been plagued throughout my boyhood by middle-aged men who mistook me for basketball material. I managed to avoid actual team sign-up sheets all through junior high school, but during my first senior high-school gym class Coach Odarizzi took me aside and said, "Ward, with that height you could go places. Why don't you take your glasses off and live a little?"

Somehow I found the coach's call to action irresistible. While I was not about to dispose of my glasses (which were crucial to any slim hope of success I might have had) I did in fact show up for the first junior-varsity practice that year.

After the usual setting-up exercises, we were instructed as to our first passing pattern. Three of us were to stand side by side at the starting line, the man in the middle holding the ball. When the whistle blew, each man was to weave in among the others, throwing the ball to the man passing directly in front. I am still a little shaky on how it was supposed to work. I guess it was like braiding, or maybe square dancing. In any case, I was in one of the first trios, and when the whistle blew and I was passed the ball I kind of zigzagged across the court in no particular pattern, throwing the ball at whoever was handy. I think at one point I threw the ball into the air and caught it myself, but I may be imagining that. In any case, after I had crossed the court in this fashion I continued to jog into the locker room, got dressed, went home, and never showed up for practice again.

I never could chin myself. Still can't, without taking a little leap to start with, which is cheating. Chinning was part of our high school physical fitness test, and when my turn came (we were to chin ourselves as many times as we could in thirty seconds) I would jump up, grab hold of the bar, and just hang there, for all intents and purposes, until my time ran out, or my hands slipped, or Coach Odarizzi told me to give it up.

"Work on that, Ward," he'd mutter, jotting something on his clipboard. Perhaps "jotting" is not the word for it, the coach was a laborious penman and tended to bite down on his tongue as he wrote.

I suppose Richard Walters, who was almost a hundred pounds overweight, had a harder time of it than I did. He would spend his thirty seconds jumping up and down beneath the bar in a vain effort to reach it, as the coach solemnly stood by with his stop watch.

We usually kicked off gym class by climbing ropes to the gymnasium ceiling. I was started off on the smooth, knotless ropes, but after a few floor-bound, rope-burned days I was shown to the one knotted rope, before which I cued up with the anemic, the obese, and the cowardly, who could not have made it up a ladder, let alone a rope.

I would grab hold of the rope and then, as I dangled, try to get it tangled with my legs. Within seconds, I would get this draining feeling in my arms and down I would slide to the floor, folding up like a spider. The coach sometimes said I wasn't trying, but he never noticed how the pits of my elbows hollowed during rope climbing, sure evidence of my exertion.

I don't think I was ever the very last to be chosen for gym class teams, but I was usually among the last three or four. This group included Richard Walters, who had about as much trouble getting around as chinning, a nearly blind boy named Merritt Hull who was always losing school days to a urinary-tract disorder, and an eruptive menace named Norenski, who frequently fell into rages, kicking at groins when anyone tried to tell him what to do. By the time the choice was narrowed down to this foursome, one of the captains would say, "What the hell, at least he's tall," and I'd be chosen.

I still don't know what "offsides" means, and I avoid all games in which the term is used. I played soccer once in summer camp, but only because I had to, and every few days someone would shout that I was offsides. I would always apologize profusely, and stomp around kicking at the turf, but I never knew what they were talking about.

Football huddles were a source of mystery and confusion for me. There would always be a short, feisty character who called the plays. I rarely had much of a role in these plays, and usually wound up somewhere on the line, half-heartedly shoving somebody around.

But I do remember a time when, in a desperation move, the captain selected me to go out for a long one. I guess the reasoning was that no one on the opposing team would have ever suspected me of such a thing. I was told, in the odoriferous hush of the huddle, that I was to break formation on 24, try a lateral cutback on 47, head forward on hike, and then plunket closed quarters in a weaving "T" down the straightaway. That may not have been the precise terminology, but it might as well have been.

I think I ran in place on 24, turned 360 degrees on 47, was totally ignored on hike, ran a little way, and then turned in time to see both teams, it seemed, piling on top of the quarterback, who was shrieking, "Where are you? Where are you?" I suppose if I had gotten hold of the ball we might have managed a first down, but I don't know what that means, either.

The first gym teacher I remember was a soft-spoken and great-jawed man named Mr. Bobbins. Mr. Bobbins took me under his wing when I showed up in the middle of the seventh grade, the new kid from India. It was basketball season when I arrived, and the class was already pounding up and down the court, shooting hoops. "The idea here, Andy," Mr. Bobbins said when I confessed my ignorance of the game, "is to put the ball through the basket."

I had known that much, but found Mr. Bobbins so reassuring that I asked, "From the top or from underneath?"

"Definitely from the top," Mr. Bobbins replied gravely. "You won't get anywhere the other way."

My gym suits fit me only in sports-shop fitting rooms. By the time I got them to school they'd be

several sizes too small. I don't think I ever passed a
happy hour in a gym suit, and at no time was I
unhappier than during the week we had coed gymnastics. All the equipment was set up in the girls'
gym, and I guess the Phys. Ed. department figured it
would be logistically too difficult to have the boys
and girls trade gyms for a couple of weeks. I prefer
to believe that this arrangement was unavoidable,
that no one thought it was a good idea. Nowhere
was I flatter of foot, spindlier and paler of leg, more
equivocal of shoulder, and heavier of acned brow
than in the girls' gymnasium.

We would have to line up boy-girl-boy-girl in
front of the parallel bars, and it was no picnic when
my turn came. I could never straighten my arms on
the parallel bars, and spent a lot of time swinging
from my armpits and making exertive noises. Another exercise involved jumping over horses. We
were supposed to run up to the things, grab them by
their handles, and swing our legs over. This, it
seemed to me, was an unreasonable expectation,
and I always balked on my approach. "You're always balking on your approach," the girls' gym
teacher would shout at me. "Don't balk on your
approach." Thus lacking momentum, I would manage only to grab the bars and kind of climb over the
things with my knees. My only comfort was in
watching Richard Walters try to clear the horse,
which he never did, even by climbing.

The balance beam was probably the least threatening piece of equipment as far as I was concerned.
I had a fair sense of balance and enormous, clutch-

ing feet, and I could usually make it across all right. But when the exercise called for straddling, and my flaring shorts endangered coed decorum, I would pretend to slip from the balance beam and then hurry to the next piece of equipment.

Coed gymnastics was in some ways a mixed bag, for while there was always the agony of failing miserably and almost nakedly before the fair sex (as it was known at the time), we were afforded chances to observe the girls exercising in their turbulent Danskins. I hope I'll never forget how Janet Gibbs moved along the balance beam, how Denise Dyktor bounced upon the trampoline, how Carol Dower arched and somersaulted across the tumbling mats. Perhaps one of the true high points of my adolescence was spotting for Suzie Hawley, who had the most beautiful, academically disruptive calves in Greenwich High School, and who happened once to slip from the high bar into my startled and grateful clutches.

But that was a fleeting delight in a context of misery. Mostly I remember just standing around, or ducking from the end of one line to the end of another, evading the mortifications of coed gymnastics as best I could.

Wrestling class was held in the cellar of the high school on gray, dusty plastic mats. Perhaps it was the cellar that made these classes seem clandestine, like cock fights. We were all paired up according to weight. I think at one point I was six feet two inches and weighed 130 pounds, and I was usually paired up with five-foot two-inch 130-pounders, rippling little dynamos who fought with savage intensity. I would often start off a match by collapsing into a last-ditch defensive posture, spread-eagled on my belly, clutching at the mat. That way, no matter how much Napoleonic might was brought to bear on flipping me over for a pin, one of my outstretched limbs would prevent it. I remember when one of my opponents actually burst into tears, because every time he managed to fold one of my limbs into an operable bundle, out would flop another, too distant to reach without letting go of the first. I may never have won a match this way, but at least I lost on points, not pins.

For eleven years, Physical Education had been an agony, but in my senior year I finally realized that I couldn't do any worse in it by not trying than I had done by trying. I took it upon myself to lighten things up when it seemed to me that everyone was getting worked up over nothing. I'd wink at opposing linesmen, do Gillette commercials between plays, stuff the ball under my shirt and accuse my teammates of getting me into trouble.

None of this went over well with the athletes among us, nor with Coach Odarizzi. "Knock it off, Ward," he'd call from the sidelines. "And grow up."

Playing games still comes up from time to time, and when it does, some of the old miseries return. I pass a couple of friends who are shooting baskets on an outdoor court. "Hey, Ward," one of them shouts.

"Come on, Stretch. Let's see what you can do." I have mastered the weary shrug, the scornful wave, the hurried departure. But the ball is tossed my way—deftly, by a man who comes to my shoulders —before I can escape.

I make a pawing motion to gather it toward me, try to trap it in the hollow of my stomach. It rolls down my clamped legs, bounces upon one of my size fourteens, rolls listlessly away. I reach for it with a clapping movement, capture it between my palms, straighten up and sigh.

"O.K., Ace," someone shouts, "swish it in there."

"It's been a while," I say, giving the ball a tentative bounce. I squint over the top of the ball, regard the distant basket, hold my breath, and at last, with a hunching lunge, throw the goddamn thing.

It takes a direct route to the rim of the hoop, which makes a chattering noise on contact and sends the ball back in a high arc over my head. "Man," I say, lurching after it, "am I out of practice."

Better Read than Dead: A Revised Opinion
Fran Liebowitz

My attendance at grammar school coincided rather unappealingly with the height of the cold war. This resulted in my spending a portion of each day sitting cross-legged, head in lap, either alone under my desk or, more sociably, against the wall in the corridor. When not so occupied I could be found sitting in class reading avidly about the horrors of life under Communism. I was not a slow child, but I believed passionately that Communists were a race of horned men who divided their time equally between the burning of Nancy Drew books and the devising of a plan of nuclear attack that would land the largest and most lethal bomb squarely upon the third-grade class of Thomas Jefferson School in Morristown, New Jersey. This was a belief widely held among my classmates and it was reinforced daily by teachers and those parents who were of the Republican persuasion.

Among the many devices used to keep this belief alive was a detailed chart that appeared yearly in our social studies book. This chart pointed out the severe economic hardships of Communist life. The reading aloud of the chart was accompanied by a running commentary from the teacher and went something like this:

"This chart shows how long a man must work in Russia in order to purchase the following goods. We then compare this to the length of time it takes a man in the United States to earn enough money to purchase the same goods."

RUSSIA	U.S.A.
A PAIR OF SHOES— 38 HOURS "And they only have brown oxfords in Russia, so that nobody ever gets to wear shoes without straps even for dress-up. Also they have never even heard of Capezios, and if they did, no one would be allowed to wear them because they all have to work on farms whenever they are not busy making atom bombs."	A PAIR OF SHOES— 2 HOURS "And we have all kinds of shoes, even Pappagallos."

RUSSIA	U.S.A.

A LOAF OF BREAD— 2½ HOURS

"They do not have peanut butter in Russia, or Marshmallow Fluff, but their bread has a lot of crust on it, which they force all the children to eat."

A LOAF OF BREAD— 5 MINUTES

"We have cinnamon raisin bread and english muffins and we can put whatever we like on it because we have democracy."

A POUND OF NAILS— 6 HOURS

"And they need a lot of nails in Russia because everyone has to work very hard all the time building things—even mothers."

A POUND OF NAILS— 8 MINUTES

"Even though we don't need that many nails because we have Scotch tape and staples."

A STATION WAGON— 9 YEARS

"If they were even permitted to own them, which they are not, so everyone has to walk everywhere even though they are very tired from building so many things like atom bombs."

A STATION WAGON— 4 MONTHS

"And we have so many varieties to choose from— some painted to look like wood on the sides and some that are two different colors. We also have lots of other cars, such as convertible sports cars."

A PAIR OF OVERALLS— 11 HOURS

"And everyone has to wear overalls all the time and they're all the same color so nobody gets to wear straight skirts even if they're in high school."

A PAIR OF OVERALLS— 1 HOUR

"But since we can choose what we want to wear in a democracy, mostly farmers wear overalls and they like to wear them."

A DOZEN EGGS— 7 HOURS

"But they hardly ever get to eat them because eggs are a luxury in Russia and there

A DOZEN EGGS— 9 MINUTES

"We have lots of eggs here and that is why we can have eggnog, egg salad, even

RUSSIA	U.S.A.
are no luxuries under Communism."	Easter eggs, except for the Jewish children in the class, who I'm sure have something just as nice on their holiday which is called Hanukkah."
A TELEVISION SET— 2 YEARS "But they don't have them. That's right, they do not have TV in Russia because they know that if the people in Russia were allowed to watch *Leave It to Beaver* they would all want to move to the United States, and probably most of them would want to come to Morristown."	**A TELEVISION SET— 2 WEEKS** "Any many people have two television sets and some people like Dougie Bershey have color TV so that he can tell everyone in class what color everything was on *Walt Disney*."

All of this was duly noted by both myself and my classmates, and the vast majority of us were rather right-wing all through grammar school. Upon reaching adolescence, however, a number of us rebelled and I must admit to distinctly leftist leanings during my teen years. Little by little, though, I have been coming around to my former way of thinking and, while I am not all that enamored of our local form of government, I have reacquired a marked distaste for Theirs.

My political position is based largely on my aversion to large groups, and if there's one thing I know about Communism it's that large groups are definitely in the picture. I do not work well with others and I do not wish to learn to do so. I do not even dance well with others if there are too many of them, and I have no doubt but that Communist discotheques are hideously overcrowded. "From each according to his ability, to each according to his needs" is not a decision I care to leave to politicians, for I do not believe that an ability to remark humorously on the passing scene would carry much weight with one's comrades or that one could convince them of the need for a really reliable answering service. The common good is not my cup of tea—it is the uncommon good in which I am interested, and I do not deceive myself that such statements are much admired by the members of farming collectives. Communists all seem to wear small caps, a look I consider better suited to tubes of toothpaste than to people. We number, of course, among us our own cap wearers, but I assure you they are easily avoided. It is my understanding that Communism requires of its adherents that they arise early and participate in a strenuous round of calisthenics. To someone who wishes that cigarettes came already lit the thought of such exertion at any hour when decent people are just nodding off is thoroughly abhorrent. I have been further advised that in the Communist world an aptitude for speaking or writing in an amusing fashion doesn't count for spit. I therefore have every intention of doing my best to keep the Iron Curtain from being drawn across Fifty-seventh Street. It is to this end that I have prepared a little chart of my own for the edification of my fellow New Yorkers.

The following chart compares the amount of time

it takes a Communist to earn enough to purchase the following goods against the amount of time it takes a New Yorker to do the same.

COMMUNIST	NEW YORKER
A CO-OP APARTMENT IN THE EAST SEVENTIES ON THE PARK—4,000 YEARS. And even then you have to share it with the rest of the collective. There is not a co-op in the city with that many bathrooms.	A CO-OP APARTMENT IN THE EAST SEVENTIES ON THE PARK—No time at all if you were lucky in the parent department. If you have not been so blessed it could take as long as twenty years, but at least you'd have your own bathroom.
A SUBSCRIPTION TO *The New Yorker*—3 WEEKS. And even then it is doubtful that you'd understand the cartoons.	A SUBSCRIPTION TO *The New Yorker*—1 HOUR, maybe less, because in a democracy one frequently receives such things as gifts.
A FIRST-CLASS AIRPLANE TICKET TO PARIS—6 MONTHS—Paris, Comrade? Not so fast.	A FIRST-CLASS AIRPLANE TICKET TO PARIS—Varies widely, but any smart girl can acquire such a ticket with ease if she plays her cards right.
A FERNANDO SANCHEZ NIGHTGOWN—3 MONTHS. With the cap? Very attractive.	A FERNANDO SANCHEZ NIGHTGOWN—1 WEEK, less if you know someone in the business, and need I point out that your chances of being so connected are far greater in a democracy such as ours than they are in Peking.
DINNER AT A FINE RESTAURANT—2 YEARS to earn the money; 27 years for the collective to decide on a resturant.	DINNER AT A FINE RESTAURANT—No problem if one has chosen one's friends wisely.

A Scholastic Schism
Phyllis Naylor

Somebody should make me superintendent of schools for a week and I'd make some curriculum changes you wouldn't believe. For one thing, I would have math problems that resembled real life: instead of counting how many pencils in five gross (did you ever buy a gross of anything?), I would have kids figuring out how many Good Humor bars it would cost them if they had just broken a garage window and would have to forfeit their allowance of forty-five cents for twenty-one weeks. Instead of memorizing the layers of the earth's crust, I would have them memorize the numbers of all the interstate highways within a fifty-mile radius. And rather than have them study sentence structure, I would give them a course in communication, which would emphasize speaking without profanity, listening without interruption, and developing the ability to reflect upon the other person's point of view.

I would make sure that no kid graduated from high school until he had learned to change a light bulb and replace a fuse. I'd make a diploma conditional upon learning to run all three cycles on the washing machine and finding the serial number on the dryer. Students of the Naylor System would have to know that Bach was a composer, not a candy manufacturer, and that Renoir was not the trade name for a hair spray.

My students would have to know how to buy a plane ticket and switch flights in Denver. They'd have to be able to use their own two legs to walk to the library and do something more in the kitchen than defrost pizza and a little Sara Lee. There would be field trips to the hospital emergency rooms to see what somebody looks like after a motorcycle accident, and they'd learn to bend, fold, and mutilate computer payment cards when the bill was wrong and they couldn't get anyone's attention.

I don't know if my school would be accredited. I don't know if my students would ever make it to college. But I'll bet there wouldn't be a single one of them jumping out of a ten-story window when he was forty years old because he couldn't cope.

Anticipating Pain
Phyllis Naylor

When Susan began junior high school, she came home to report that some day soon there would be a "Seventh-Grade Sing Day." Then she went up to her room and bawled.

We finally got to the facts: all seventh-graders were supposedly taught the school song at a pep rally. The junior-high basketball team hoped that all the new students would show up for the first game, cheering madly and singing with gusto, and it was to this end that Seventh-Grade Sing Day had come into being. On this day it was the privilege of any eighth- or ninth-grader to stop new students in the hall and demand that they sing the school song. All sorts of punishments and humiliations were supposedly in store for those who did not comply—as though being backed up against the wall and asked to sing solo was not humiliation enough.

What do I do? I wondered, and knew, as soon as I'd asked, that the answer was *nothing.* Much as a mama might like, she does not go to the principal and demand that the tradition be stopped. She does not follow her daughter around school on the appointed day to help ward off evil. And she does not give in to the cowardly impulse to keep her daughter home.

I remember my freshman year of high school. It was torturous not because of what happened, which was nothing, but because of what we expected. We had been told that some time during our freshman year, all the senior boys would storm the girls' locker room during gym and steal whatever they could find—a wholesale panty raid. Of course, it never happened, and never had, but for an entire year we girls would rush to the showers like lemmings to the sea, clutching our towels around us and praying we could get there and back, before the seniors arrived.

There was little I could do for Susan except treat the whole thing lightly and urge her to do the same. With Susan, however, this was impossible. Every night she would go to her room and practice the song over and over. Each morning she would set out, books in her arms, resignation on her face, and I would ache for the hurt she was feeling. The big day was set only to be postponed. The worst was always yet to come.

And finally, one day, it happened. One day when I was busy with other things and had forgotten to ache, Susan burst in, collapsed on the sofa, and said, "It's over!"

You would have thought she'd just had her tonsils out or climbed a mountain, at least. I sank down gratefully beside her to hear all the gory details.

It's unfair, you know. Each of my kids has to go through it only once: I've got to experience it again with Jack and Peter.

CAMPUS CAPERS

~~~~~~

Spring Bulletin
Woody Allen

~~~~~~

The number of college bulletins and adult-education come-ons that keep turning up in my mailbox convinces me that I must be on a special mailing list for dropouts. Not that I'm complaining; there is something about a list of extension courses that piques my interest with a fascination hitherto reserved for a catalogue of Hong Kong honeymoon accessories, sent to me once by mistake. Each time I read through the latest bulletin of extension courses, I make immediate plans to drop everything and return to school. (I was ejected from college many years ago, the victim of unproved accusations not unlike those once attached to Yellow Kid Weil.) So far, however, I am still an uneducated, unextended adult, and I have fallen into the habit of browsing through an imaginary, handsomely printed course bulletin that is more or less typical of them all:

SUMMER SESSION

Economic Theory: A systematic application and critical evaluation of the basic analytic concepts of economic theory, with an emphasis on money and why it's good. Fixed coefficient production functions, cost and supply curves, and nonconvexity comprise the first semester, with the second semester concentrating on spending, making change, and keeping a neat wallet. The Federal Reserve System is analyzed, and advanced students are coached in the proper method of filling out a deposit slip. Other topics include: Inflation and Depression—how to dress for each. Loans, interest, welching.

History of European Civilization: Ever since the discovery of a fossilized eohippus in the men's washroom at Siddon's Cafeteria in East Rutherford, New Jersey, it has been suspected that at one time Europe and America were connected by a strip of land that later sank or became East Rutherford, New Jersey, or both. This throws a new perspective on the formation of European society and enables historians to conjecture about why it sprang up in an area that would have made a much better Asia. Also studied in the course is the decision to hold the Renaissance in Italy.

Introduction to Psychology: The theory of human behavior. Why some men are called "lovely individuals" and why there are others you just want to pinch. Is there a split between mind and body, and, if so, which is better to have? Aggression and rebellion are discussed. (Students particularly interested in these aspects of psychology are advised to take one of these Winter Term courses: Introduction to Hostility; Intermediate Hostility; Advanced Hatred; Theoretical Foundations of Loathing.) Special consideration is given to a study of consciousness as opposed to unconsciousness, with many helpful hints on how to remain conscious.

Psychopathology: Aimed at understanding obsessions and phobias, including the fear of being suddenly captured and stuffed with crabmeat, reluctance to return a volleyball serve, and the inability to say the word "mackinaw" in the presence of women. The compulsion to seek out the company of beavers is analyzed.

Philosophy I: Everyone from Plato to Camus is read, and the following topics are covered:

Ethics: The categorical imperative, and six ways to make it work for you.

Aesthetics: Is art the mirror of life, or what?

Metaphysics: What happens to the soul after death? How does it manage?

Epistemology: Is knowledge knowable? If not, how do we know this?

The Absurd: Why existence is often considered

silly, particularly for men who wear brown-and-white shoes. Manyness and oneness are studied as they relate to otherness. (Students achieving oneness will move ahead to twoness.)

Philosophy XXIX-B: Introduction to God. Confrontation with the Creator of the universe through informal lectures and field trips.

The New Mathematics: Standard mathematics has recently been rendered obsolete by the discovery that for years we have been writing the numeral five backward. This has led to a reëvaluation of counting as a method of getting from one to ten. Students are taught advanced concepts of Boolean Algebra, and formerly unsolvable equations are dealt with by threats of reprisals.

Fundamental Astronomy: A detailed study of the universe and its care and cleaning. The sun, which is made of gas, can explode at any moment, sending our entire planetary system hurtling to destruction; students are advised what the average citizen can do in such a case. They are also taught to identify various constellations, such as the Big Dipper, Cygnus the Swan, Sagittarius the Archer, and the twelve stars that form Lumides the Pants Salesman.

Modern Biology: How the body functions, and where it can usually be found. Blood is analyzed, and it is learned why it is the best possible thing to have coursing through one's veins. A frog is dissected by students and its digestive tract is compared with man's, with the frog giving a good account of itself except on curries.

Rapid Reading: This course will increase reading speed a little each day until the end of the term, by which time the student will be required to read *The Brothers Karamazov* in fifteen minutes. The method is to scan the page and eliminate everything except pronouns from one's field of vision. Soon the pronouns are eliminated. Gradually the student is encouraged to nap. A frog is dissected. Spring comes. People marry and die. Pinkerton does not return.

Musicology III: The Recorder. The student is taught how to play "Yankee Doodle" on this end-blown wooden flute, and progresses rapidly to the Brandenburg Concertos. Then slowly back to "Yankee Doodle."

Music Appreciation: In order to "hear" a great piece of music correctly, one must: (1) know the birthplace of the composer, (2) be able to tell a rondo from a scherzo, and back it up with action. Attitude is important. Smiling is bad form unless the composer has intended the music to be funny, as in *Till Eulenspiegel,* which abounds in musical jokes (although the trombone has the best lines). The ear, too, must be trained, for it is our most easily deceived organ and can be made to think it is a nose by bad placement of stereo speakers. Other topics include: The four-bar rest and its potential as a political weapon. The Gregorian Chant: Which monks kept the beat.

Writing for the Stage: All drama is conflict. Character development is also very important. Also what they say. Students learn that long, dull speeches are not so effective, while short, "funny" ones seem to go over well. Simplified audience psychology is explored: Why is a play about a lovable old character named Gramps often not as interesting in the theatre as staring at the back of someone's head and trying to make him turn around? Interesting aspects of stage history are also examined. For example, before the invention of italics, stage directions were often mistaken for dialogue, and great actors frequently found themselves saying, "John rises, crosses left." This naturally led to embarrassment and, on some occasions, dreadful notices. The phenomenon is analyzed in detail, and students are guided in avoiding mistakes. Required text: A. F. Shulte's *Shakespeare: Was He Four Women?*

Introduction to Social Work: A course designed to instruct the social worker who is interested in going out "in the field." Topics covered include: how to organize street gangs into basketball teams, and vice versa; playgrounds as a means of preventing juvenile crime, and how to get potentially homicidal cases to try the sliding pond; discrimination; the broken home; what to do if you are hit with a bicycle chain.

Yeats and Hygiene, A Comparative Study: The poetry of William Butler Yeats is analyzed against a background of proper dental care. (Course open to a limited number of students.)

Freshman Adviser
George Boas

We are sitting pencil in hand, surrounded by college catalogues, rules and regulations, directories, handbooks, mimeographed slips with last-minute changes of courses on them, folders with big cards for the students' records, pads with two carbons on which to write out schedules. We are all washed and clean, fresh from a summer in which we were supposed to rest and which we spent making enough money to fill out the gap between our salaries and a living wage. We are all resigned to the winter that is before us, teaching, coal bills, committee meetings, those tonsils of Susie's, academic freedom, subscription to the Symphony, student activities, what price a decent pair of shoes. . . . We smile at each other and sigh at the mass of paper. We have never learned all the rules. How can anyone learn them? Different ones for students in the college of arts and sciences, pre-meds, engineers. But what are rules anyway?

Here they come. . . .

His name is Rosburgh van Stiew. One can see he is one of the Van Stiews—and if one can't, he'll let one know soon enough. That suit of fuzzy tweed, that regimental cravat, that custom-made shirt. Right out of *Vanity Fair*. Already he has the Phi Pho Phum pledge button in his buttonhole.

He speaks with a drawl. It is the voice of his mother's *face-à-main*. He has slightly wavy blond hair—his mother still has a crinkly white pompadour, like Queen Mary's. He has weary eyes.

No use to smile.

"Very well, Mr. Van Stiew. Have you any idea of the courses you'd like to take?"

"No . . . aren't there some things you sort of have to take?"

"Freshman English and Gym."

"Well, I may as well take them."

"History?"

"Do you have to?"

"No. You can take Philosophy, Political Science, or Economics instead."

Mr. Van Stiew tightens his cravat.

"Guess I'll take History."

"Ancient or Modern?"

"Well—when do they come?"

"Modern at 8:30, Wednesdays, Thursdays, and Saturdays; Ancient at 9:30, Mondays, Tuesdays, and Wednesdays."

"Oh, Ancient."

Mr. Van Stiew looks shocked that one should have asked.

One shouldn't have.

"Very well, Ancient History."

That leaves three more courses.

"One of the fellows said to take Art Appreciation."

"Yes, you could do that. But sooner or later you are required to take French and German and a laboratory science."

"Couldn't I put them off until next year?"

"You can until you're a senior."

"I think I'll put them off then. I don't want too heavy a schedule."

"Mathematics?"

"Do I have to?"

"It all depends. What are you going to major in?"

"Do I have to major?"

"More or less."

"When do I have to decide?"

"Next year."

So it goes with Mr. Van Stiew. He is using his right of election, his free will. His personality must not be crushed. He will have a Liberal Education, be a member of the Tennis Team, the Dramatic Club, and manager of the Glee Club. And as a prominent alumnus, he will see to it that the Football Team is never oppressed by a fastidious faculty.

Enter Mr. William Hogarth.

Hogarth is from the city Technical High School. Engineer. Red hair, freckles. Ready-made blue serge.

"Math, Physics, Philosophy, German—why can't I take Chemistry too? I'll make up my French this summer. . . . No, can't take any Saturday classes, working at the Universal Clothing Outlet Saturdays."

"English Literature?"

"Do I have to? . . . All right, Professor, put it down. Where do I get my text books? Don't they have any second-hand ones? . . . Classes begin tomorrow? All right. . . . Yes, I know about the Physical Exam. Had it already. . . . No, I guess I know everything now."

"If you need any information, Mr. Hogarth, I'm in my—"

"Thanks, don't believe I will."

He's gone.

Woof! One lights a cigarette.

A presence is before one, grinning. Lots of yellow hair parted in the middle, rising on each side of the part and falling like too ripe wheat. Head slightly to one side. Very red face.

Timidly shoves forward receipted bill from the Treasurer's Office.

Fred Wilkinson.

Mr. Wilkinson doesn't know what he's going to major in as yet—"you see, I may not stay here four years." A glance at his high-school record makes that more than probable.

"English and Physical Training, that is, Gym."

"Can't I be excused from that?"

"Have you a physical disability?"

"I'm not sure . . ."

"Well, we'll put it down anyway and you can talk it over with the doctor."

"French? German?"

"I'm not very good on languages."

"Mathematics?"

"Heavens, no!"

"Philosophy?"

"What's that?"

"It's—it's part of the business of philosophy to find out, Mr. Wilkinson."

One stops in time.

"I don't believe you'd like Philosophy. Physics? You have to take one science."

"Isn't there one where you take a trip in the spring?"

"Geology?"

"Is that where you study rocks and things?"

"Yes." God forgive me.

"I guess I'll take that."

"History?"

Quick response. The eyes actually grow bright.

"Oh, yes, History. My brother said to take History."

"Good, that's that anyway. . . . Ancient or Modern?"

"A—what?"

"Ancient or Modern?"

Mr. Wilkinson looks as if he were going to cry. His lower lip seems to swell. His eyes blink. But he is only thinking.

"Which do you study Keats and Shelley in?"

"Which History course?"

"Yes. My brother studied Keats and Shelley. That's the course I want. Don't they come in History?"

"They are undoubtedly a part of history" (one grows pontifical) "but I don't believe they usually are discussed in the History courses."

"I'm sure my brother studied them here."

"Maybe it was the History of English Literature."

"Would that have Keats and Shelley?"

"I imagine so."

Mr. Wilkinson is dubious.

"Well, I tell you, Professor. Couldn't you put it down, and then if it isn't all right maybe I could change it afterwards. I could change it, couldn't I, you know, if I didn't like it, if they didn't teach Keats and Shelley in it? I could change it, couldn't I?"

Why not? Mr. Wilkinson will flunk out at midterm anyway.

So we go.

The pad of the three carbons grows thinner and thinner. The atmosphere grows thicker and thicker. The advisers grow stupider and stupider. The day grows shorter and shorter. By night all schedules are made. To-morrow classes will begin. And after tomorrow Mr. Van Stiew, Mr. Hogarth, Mr. Wilkinson, and the rest will begin dropping courses, adding courses, shifting courses about until they have left of their original schedules only English Literature and Gym which are required in the Freshman year.

The Apple Polisher
(Nulla fides fronti)*
Richard Armour

Unless the seating is alphabetical and its name begins with some letter other than *A* or *B*, the Apple Polisher sits on the front row. It is not that its hearing is poor but that it wishes to see and, above all, to be seen. In fact it wishes to be seen so closely that each expression of interest, understanding, and adulation will be observed by the Professor.

The Apple Polisher does not actually polish apples. This is what is known in Academe as a Figure of Speech. The Apple Polisher may have given pol-

*No trust in the countenance. I.e., looks can be deceiving (and so also can words).

ished apples to the teacher in High School, but now it brings other gifts. If a male, it may bring nothing but an attentive, admiring look, meanwhile cocking an ear* so as not to miss a word of the Professor's lecture, even while thinking of something else. If it is a female, it depends less on the ear than on other parts of the anatomy.

The Apple Polisher is inclined to fawn. If it were a real fawn it would rub its soft fur against the Professor's leg and lick the Professor's hand, meanwhile looking up endearingly with its soft brown eyes. Its purpose is to make the Professor look upon it with tenderness and affection, as well as to inflate the Professor's ego, even though it is already inflated almost to the bursting point. Only in this way can the Apple Polisher get a grade of A or B instead of the C or D it deserves.

Occasionally a Professor is aware of the intentions of the Apple Polisher and tries to lecture to the Average Students in the middle rows and the Somnolent Students in the back row. It may have its attention called to the front row from time to time, however, if the female Student with what is known as Cleavage drops its pencil. When it stoops to pick it up, the Professor, despite a Supreme Effort of Will, drops its eyes. No matter how tired its eyes are from reading papers and examinations, they rise, or lower, to the occasion.†

---

*Unlike a pistol, an ear makes no distracting click when it is cocked.
†As a consequence the Professor may think better (and more often) of the Student.

What the Apple Polisher fails to realize is that it is in Academe not to polish anything but to acquire polish. That, however, is a Subtle Distinction, better left to the Philologists and the Philosophers.

~~~~~~

The Athlete
(Genus musculum)
Richard Armour

~~~~~~

The Athlete* is probably the largest, strongest creature in Academe. It is so heavy it has to be supported by an Athletic Scholarship, which is not to be confused with an Athletic Supporter.

Everything about the Athlete is athletic. It has, for instance, not only Athlete's Foot but Athlete's Head, the latter not helped by any powder or lotion. It also has enormous muscles it flexes from time to time, partly to develop them further and partly to impress those creatures of Academe, such as the

*Often pronounced "Athalete" by those who find it hard to say "thl." The medical term *thlipsis* is difficult even for an M.D.

wear, it tries to leave an opening so that some of Grind and the Phi Bete, which have no observable musculature.

The Athlete may be either male or female. However, the male Athlete has more appeal to the average female than the female Athlete has to the average male. The male Athlete is much admired for its hairy chest. No matter what athletic costume it may this hair will show.

Some believe the Athlete is out of place in Academe and belongs in the Animal Kingdom. This is perhaps because of its resemblance to such animals as the Bear and the Gorilla, both being muscular and hairy. It is sometimes asked, "What brought the Athlete to Academe?" The answer is that it was probably the Admission or the Coach that sought out the Athlete and waved an Athletic Scholarship under its nose. Though protected by a nose guard, the Athlete caught the scent and lost consciousness. Upon awakening it found itself in Academe, among such strange creatures as the Intellectual and the Brain.

Unlike the Bear, the Athlete hibernates at odd times, sleeping through the months when it is Out of Season and nothing is expected of it. Then the other Students of Academe, busy studying, are hardly aware of its existence. Being In Season is, to the Athlete, comparable to being In Heat in the Animal Kingdom.

Nonetheless the Athlete is of a charitable nature and makes its contribution to School Spirit and the

All-Around image. Without the Athlete, Academe would not be the same.* Also that endangered species, the Cheerleader, might become extinct.

The Athlete is especially meaningful to the Old Grad, notably the one that can remember nothing from four years in Academe but the scores in the annual Big Game.

In fairness, it should be remarked that there is nothing to keep the Athlete from becoming a Good Student or even a Rhodes Scholar. In fact the Athlete has a better chance to become the latter than most creatures in Academe.† Moreover, after Graduation the Athlete may become a Success, having learned in Academe, if it learned nothing else, that it is not the way you play the game that counts, it is winning.

---

*We are not saying whether better or worse.
†"Have you ever rowed?" the Selection Committee may ask. Some think the name should be changed to Rowed Scholarship, since the emphasis is as much on the scull as on the skull.

The Librarian
(*Librarius, liberalis, libertas, et cetera*)*
Richard Armour

The Librarian is related to the Bookworm.† In fact it was probably a Bookworm as a Student and unquestionably a worm of some sort in Library School. But it emerged from its vermicular state and appeared as a winged creature, resembling a butterfly or moth. Fluttering about from book to book and from reader to reader, the Librarian is careful not to move its wings too rapidly or to bat them (there are

---

*Library, liberal, liberty, and so forth. All of these words go back to the Latin *liber*, but there is a pronounced difference. The difference between *liber*, book and *liber*, free is that one has a short "i" and one has a long "i." That may be why books are free at a library but a librarian is not always free to purchase or circulate certain books.

†But not, as one might think, to the Bookkeeper, a species actually hated by the Librarian.

those who think some Librarians *are* Bats) against anything, lest it make a Noise.

A Noise* is what it abhors most, especially in that sacred area of the Library known as the Reading Room. There the loudest sound heard is the Librarian's "Shh!" a sibilant stricture that resembles a sudden gust of wind or a wave subsiding sensuously on the sandy seashore. The comparison with a wave is probably more apt, since the Librarian's "Shh!" usually drowns out the whispers, chair scrapings, coughs, and gum-poppings of Readers.

The Librarian, whether male or female, is almost always in love. It is not in love with other Librarians, though it likes them well enough, but with Books. Often, becoming a Bibliophile, it projects its dainty feelers and voluptuously feels a Volume from its jacket to its flyleaf and from its frontispiece to its End. It may even reach in and touch its Appendix. The satisfaction it gets is beyond description and therefore will not be described here.

What disturbs the Librarian almost as much as a Noise is finding a book that has been mistreated or, even worse, misplaced—wrongly shelved by some do-it-yourshelf reader. Of course the Librarian itself may deflower a book, removing a flower that has been pressed or used as a bookmark. Such a book may in addition be Overdue.

The Librarian silently flits about from the Card Catalog, which is used to catalog cards, to the Stacks. The latter are not really stacks, since books

---

*Also known, by the Librarian, as a Racket or a Disturbance.

are not stacked but neatly placed on shelves side by side. If they were actually stacked in stacks in the Stacks, no creature in Academe would be so distressed as the Librarian.*

With reference to the Librarian, we should not overlook the Reference Librarian. This is a species of Librarian that flourishes on Tracking Things Down and is so good at Sources that it is thought to be a magician or Sourcerer.

Finally there is the Rare Book Librarian that, devouring books, likes them rare. Oddly, most books that are rare are also well-done. *De gustibus non est disputandum,* or for this reason there is no accounting for the taste.†

---

*The Librarian, if a female, may itself be well stacked.
†According to Francis Bacon, "Some books are to be tasted, others swallowed, and some few to be chewed and digested." As the Librarian knows, books that are swallowed but neither chewed nor digested can cause trouble, especially those that are bound in leather or buckram.

~~~~~~

The Tuition
(Absque argento omnia vana)*
Richard Armour

~~~~~~

One seldom mentions the Tuition without also mentioning its close friends and constant companions, Room and Board. The only time the three are not found together is when a Student lives Off Campus and then is concerned only with the Tuition. The name of the Tuition comes from the Latin verb *tueri, tuitus, tutus,* to watch, guard, protect. Thus in a sense, and sometimes innocence, it is money paid by the Student's parents to see that the Student is kept out of trouble, or put away for four years.†

---

*Without money all efforts are in vain. Higher education keeps getting higher, but it is still possible for the rich to get a poor education.
†It may be only a coincidence that the term "term" is used both in Academe and in prison.

But the Tuition is also related to the Tutor, so that the Tuition has, or should have, something to do with teaching or being taught. However, when a Student says it "pays Tuition," it does not really pay the Tuition. It pays the Business Office, which in turn pays the Administration, the Faculty, the Grounds Force, and the Incidental Expenses. What it pays, as the Student is repeatedly told, and told again* when it becomes an Alum, is not enough to cover everything. The difference is made up by the Endowment, and a well-endowed college is very nearly as attractive as well-endowed Co-Ed.

As the Tuition grows larger and larger, its increase in size is announced in smaller and smaller type. The Incoming Student is also informed that the Tuition does not include Fees, which are small creatures that cling to the Tuition and try to escape notice. These are given such names as the Health Fee, the Lab Fee, the Late Registration Fee, and, for those that cannot be broken of the habit of playing the organ, the Practice Fee.

The Tuition can be paid in a Lump Sum, which may explain its lumpy appearance, or in Installments. Unlike empty bottles, the Tuition is not returnable, whether the Student returns or not.

The opposite of the Tuition is the Intuition. Unlike the Tuition, the Intuition is free. It comes as standard equipment with the brain, and is not an extra. Intuition is knowing something immediately, without being taught, and if it were more prevalent

---

*And again.

would mean a drastic change in Academe: Professors would no longer be necessary. Nor, in fact, would Academe. Also, since everything would be seen with the mind's eye, on which it would be difficult to fit glasses, ophthalmologists, optometrists, and opticians would be unnecessary.

Until Intuition becomes more evident, it is probably unnecessary to say that the Tuition is necessary.* Tuition is essential in Academe, the land of the Fee.

---

*Except in a State Institution. There is no Tuition in an Insane Asylum.

Between Classes
Ogden Nash

Oh, listen to the creed of one who never even
  sniffed the aroma
Of a diploma;
Oh, hark, to the philosophy of a mentally un-
  developed person (me)
Who didn't get within several probations of a
  degree;
Who departed early from the campus
Thereby breaking the hearts of his ma, his pa,
  his two grandmas and his two grandpus;
Who learned practically nothing during his so-
  journ at one of the country's prominent cul-
  tural joints
Save the following points:
First,

That debtors are swell forgebtors.
While the friend who to you money has lent
Will remember it world without ent.

Second,

That every fresh semester
Brings with it its own fresh disester.

Third,

That both sports clothes and décolleté
Look quite odd when worn by ladies of the
    fécolleté.

Fourth,

That trying to make a quarter do the work of
    a dollar
Is like trying to get a sixteen neck into a
    fifteen collar.

Fifth,

That—name of a name of a name of a name
    of a name!
One should never bet real money on even the
    most sewed-up game.

Sixth,

That debutantes are simply overjoyed
To be thought hard-boiled when as a matter
    of fact they are only Freud.

Seventh,

That most inhabitants of dormitories
Are splendid candidates for reformitories.

Eighth,

That while any attempt by an undergraduate
    to tell the truth about undergraduates is
    regarded as calumny
By furious alumny
Still, though the W.C.T.U. and the Board of

Prohibition, Temperance and Public Mor-
als to hear it will be amazed,

There is a lot more hell talked about than
raised.

Ninth,

That one's fellows rightly consider one an ass

Should one let oneself in for a nine o'clock
class—also that,

Tenth,

The most important of one's objects

Is to select one's courses from among the less
difficult sobjects.

Eleventh,

That alcohol is an intoxicant

And therefore gin can often do what Moxie
can't.

Twelfth,

That Apaches and Cherokees and Choctaws

Are nothing but amiable old S.P.C.A. agents
when compared to deans and proctaws.

Thirteenth and last,

That anybody who spends even a week at
any university and can't learn more than
this

Deserves to be locked in a miniature golf
course with one crooning Eskimo, one
epileptic Bantu, and one backgammon-
minded Swiss.

Hire Education
Art Buchwald

WASHINGTON—The Timkens sent their child Laura off to college with a check for $7,000 in tuition and thought that was the end of it. But soon after they received a letter from the Dean of Studies.

"We are happy to announce that we have instituted a remedial reading class for college freshmen and strongly advise that your daughter Laura participate in it. If she doesn't, it is our opinion that Laura will not be able to keep up with her studies. The cost will be $250."

Timken read the letter. "I thought Laura could read," he said to his wife.

"So did—. I think the problem is she can read,

but she has no comprehension of what she reads."

"What did they teach her in public school and high school?"

"I have no idea, but if the college says she needs remedial reading we better see that she gets it or $7,000 will go down the drain."

A few days later they got another letter from the dean.

"The English Department has brought to our attention the fact that your daughter Laura cannot write. They have recommended that she enroll in the remedial writing class which we started two years ago when we discovered this was a common problem for most college students. If you agree that Laura should get this special help, please send a check for $250."

Timken was now very angry.

"How did she get in college if she can't write?"

Mrs. Timken was much more sanguine about it. "Laura can write. She just can't write complete sentences."

"She went to school for 12 years and she can't write a sentence?"

"Don't you remember? They were much more interested in Laura's thoughts than they were in how she put them down. The teacher's main concern was with expanding her consciousness."

"That's hogwash," Timken said. "They made an illiterate out of my daughter."

"I believe that's a bit strong. Laura graduated with honors in analytical consciousness-raising."

"But she can't write."

"I'm sure the college can help her learn to write. After all, it is an institution of higher learning."

"So now we have to pay $250 for something they should have taught her in grammar school?"

"Don't you remember when we went to the PTA meeting years ago, and the principal said it was the school's responsibility to make good citizens out of the students, and the parents' responsibility to teach the children how to read and write? Carlton, we're the ones who failed."

Timken sent in the check, and was not surprised to find another letter waiting for him a week later.

It read: "It has come to our attention that no one in the freshman class can add, multiply, subtract or divide simple sums. We feel it is urgent that this deficiency be corrected early in a student's college career. Therefore, we are setting up a special remedial arithmetic course. The fee will be $250. If you do not want your daughter to take this course we cannot guarantee she will graduate."

Once again Timken went through the ceiling. "I thought Laura got A's in math in high school."

Mrs. Timken said, "That was conceptional math. Her courses had to do with the advanced integration of numbers. She never could add or subtract them. Don't you recall when you complained once about it and Laura's teacher told you, 'She can always learn to add and subtract when she gets to college'?"

ABOUT THE EDITORS

M. JERRY WEISS, Distinguished Service professor of communications at Jersey City State College, is a nationally known authority on communications, media, reading and language arts. He received his M. A. and Ed. D. from Teachers College, Columbia University. Dr. Weiss has worked in rural, suburban and inner-city schools as classroom teacher, college professor and school consultant. He is a past president of the College Reading Association, a past president of ALAN (Assembly on Literature for Adolescents, National Council of Teachers of English), and a past president of New Jersey Reading Association.

HELEN S. WEISS has honed her sense of humor raising four children and has been active in community and synagogue activities. She served on the Montclair Citizen's Advisory Committee for Titles One and Seven. A graduate of Greensboro (N.C.) College with majors in history and journalism, she has worked in the research library of a major television network. She is currently a freelance writer.

Bantam Book Catalog

Here's your up-to-the-minute listing of over 1,400 titles by your favorite authors.

This illustrated, large format catalog gives a description of each title. For your convenience, it is divided into categories in fiction and non-fiction—gothics, science fiction, westerns, mysteries, cookbooks, mysticism and occult, biographies, history, family living, health, psychology, art.

So don't delay—take advantage of this special opportunity to increase your reading pleasure.

Just send us your name and address and 50¢ (to help defray postage and handling costs).